The Bhumihars

Caste of Eastern India

The Bhumihars

Caste of Eastern India

Sushil Kumar Sinha

(Research Officer)

Ministry of Social Justice and Empowerment

Government of India, New Delhi

Raj Publications

New Delhi - 110002

The Bhumihars: Caste of Eastern India

First Published in 2019

₹ 595

ISBN 978-81-86208-37-3

Published by : **Raj Publications**
108, 4855/24, Ansari Road,
Daryganj, New Delhi - 110002
Tel. : 011-23250939, 09811010939
E-mail: rajpublications@yahoo.co.in

Laser Typesetting : Manpreet Computers, Delhi-110009

Printed at : Balaji Offset, Delhi

Printed in India

Contents

Preface 7

Acknowledgement 13

1. Introduction 15
2. Origin of the Caste 27
3. Socio-Economic and Cultural Dimension 53
4. Caste and Politics 83
5. Caste and Education 108
6. Bhumihars and The Kisan Sabha 117
7. Brahmarshi Samaj in India 122
8. Caste : Change and Continuity 156
9. Conclusion 170

Appendices 175

Bibliography 182

Glossary 188

Index 193

Preface

Caste in India is unique mainly because it is a composite institution, having a complex origin in the combination of geographical, historical, ethnic factors which has been operative only in India. These various factors have been the geographical isolation of India, ideas about ritual purity and pollution, beliefs in taboo, totem and the possibility of purification, the institutions of ancestor beliefs in past and future births and the theory of karma, association with occupation, economic guilds and the development of socio-religious classes with exclusive privileges etc.; All these have helped in development of caste system. Within caste system, study of a particular sub-caste or mixed caste lead to understanding of the complex system in a more better way. Behaviour of this particular caste (Bhumihar Brahman) under different circumstances and socio-economic, political situation etc., gives one insight to analyse psychological and social problems and its solution for the betterment of the caste under study.

European scholars were the first to establish a relationship with India in the 18th century and became curious about its past. Their sources of information were the Brahman priests and even more secular literature such as "*Dharmashastras*" had Brahman authors and commentators, for example the caste system — a unique feature of Indian society, and has a rigid stratification in the society relate itself to power in Indian caste system, has been described in the above literature.

The first developed civilization known as Indus Valley Civilization or Harappan Culture, dates back to 2300 B.C. By 1700 B.C., the Harappan Culture had declined and the migration of Indo-Aryans from Iran dates back to 1500 B.C., introduced new features into the cultural background of North-Western India. The ethnic composition of the people involved in these various cultures were not identical. Six main races have been revealed : The earliest was negrito and this was followed by the Proto-Australoid, Mongoloid, Mediterranean and later those associated with Aryan culture.

Rigveda: the earliest literary source which speaks of four castes were primarially composed prior to 1000 B.C., Later on other vedas were written. Similarly the two epics : Ramayana and Mahabharata are concerned with the events which took place between 1000 B.C. and 700 B.C. The historical reconstruction of Aryan life and institutions based on these literature may be of the above said period. Bhumihar Brahmans/ Babhans claims their origin from "Parasuram" (a mythological person). If it is to be believed than its origin dates back between 1000 B.C. and 700 B.C., but there is no scientific and valid evidence for this. G.S. Ghurye in his book "Caste and Races in India (1996) has also assumed that a Brahmin, wherever south or east found in India, went there with the "*gotra*" and therefore could not have proceeded there much before 600 B.C.

The actual mechanism of caste was not a formal division of society into fourfold groups. The first three castes were probably a theoretical framework evolved by the Brahmans into which they systematically arranged various professions. Combinations and permutations within the latter were inevitable and explained as originating in the intermixing of castes and also birth of sub-castes (Bhumihar Brahman is one of them). The basis and continuance of the caste system depended not on the fourfold division but on the vast-network of sub-castes which was intimately connected with occupation. Eventually the sub-caste (Jati) came to have more relevance for the day to day working of Hindu society.

Caste theories of Manu, who authored "Manava Dharmashastra" or law code was written sometimes during the first two centuries AD. He had written about sub-castes/ mixed castes in his book in general but in particular he did not spoke of the Babhans (sub-caste/ mixed caste).

During Gupta dynasty (4th-6th Century A.D.) the term Dvija began to be used increasingly for the Brahmans, and with the emergence of social reformers in 6th century. A.D. many more new sub-castes/ mixed castes sprang up due to claim of superior status and rigidity of Brahmans.

Some sub-castes(more than 5000 sub castes) claim their origin from highly respected ancestors. This tendency took place during 11th-12th century A.D., such as Kayasthas, Khatris, Gurjaras, Jats, Ahir etc. The emergence of Babhan/ Bhumihar Jati may be (probably) of this period or some later period.

The Bhumihar Mahasabha, which had been active since 1896 represented their claim for recognition and in the 1931 census they were placed below the Brahman in the Bihar list of castes.

Based on various sources mentioned above, only workable inference can be drawn regarding date of origin of this caste and not a scientific one i.e., in between 1000 B.C. - 1800 A.D. Among the upper castes, Bhumihars are 2.9% of the total population of Bihar and they have control over natural resources. The popular observation that the history of Bihar is the history of the achievements and failures of the four upper castes, i.e., Brahman, Bhumihar, Rajput and Kayasthas, is therefore, not wide off the mark.

Contents in this book has been divided into nine chapters. Introduction provide information to readers about caste system in India in general and some insight into the Bhumihar caste.

Origin of the caste chapter deals with different aspects related to origin of this caste and its position among caste system in India (four fold Varna system).

Socio-economic and cultural dimension deals with family, marriage, occupation and other social institutions through which social life exists.

In today's Indian scenario, caste and politics/ education are very much relevant and plays an important role and how caste is affecting politics and involving itself in the field of education and educational institutions, help one to study various factors related to it in depth.

Role of Bhumihars in Kisan Sabha has been discussed in the said chapter.

Castes akin to Bhumihars are spread all over India and known under different names. Their professions and social life are somewhat same with minor differences. Some of these castes have been described under the title, 'Brahmarshi Samaj in India'. And last but not the least, changes that have taken place and is still taking place has been discussed under the heading 'Caste: Change and Continuity with case study'. Some remedial measures have also been discussed under this chapter to strengthen the prospects of this caste for its continuity and betterment.

The supplementary notes at the end of the book is meant to enrich reader's knowledge and every attempt has been made to make it comprehensive. In the end glossary has also been included.

Acknowledgement

I thank to all those who has helped in providing direct or indirect information especially; Sh. Prahlad Ojha of village Baniapur and Prof. Ramvachan Sharma of village Ismailpur during my field work, and office bearers of the Swami Sahajanand Samiti, Harmu, Ranchi.

It is my pleasure to thank the Chairperson, Hon'ble Justice (Retd.) R.S. Singh, Member, Smt. Neera Shastri, colleauges in research wing and librarian of the NCBC for providing inspiration and help whenever I required it.

Words are inadequate to express my gratitude to the authors and editors whose works and reports, I have taken help of and lastly my children and wife who bear with me during my work and without whose cooperation, I could not have completed this book smoothly.

Finally, I thank to Smt. Poonam Goel of Raj Publications for taking keen interest in the publication of the book.

1

Introduction

The present study deals mainly with the Bhumihars of Bihar, Jharkhand, adjoining parts of the state and Uttar Pradesh. As is well known that this caste has mythological origin and had no place in the ancient fourfold Varna (caste) system.

It is better to understand caste dynamics in perspective of caste system which is in no way very rigid regarding vocations. No man is tied down to follow his father's occupation. The ordinary pursuits and occupations of life have now been thrown open to all in India. This has also led to the emergence of sub-castes better known as Jati in different parts of the country.

In recent years, there has been a considerable modification in caste restrictions. In the towns of Bihar (including Jharkhand) inter-dining between several castes have become common. The increase of travel by bus and rail has made it difficult to maintain the distances between castes. Losing caste on being touched by an untouchable is now a thing of the past. sub-caste marriages are now an every day affairs.

Intercaste marriages have also picked up in recent years. There has been a distinct and gradual weakening of caste sanctions. Among higher castes there is now no caste panchayat, because members are widely dispersed.

Swami Sahajanand Saraswati in his book "Brahmarshi Vansh Vistar", published in 1915 has used the term 'Brahmarshi' to include all castes akin to Bhumihar and spread over in different parts of the country as for example; Tyagi and Bhumihar of U.P./ Delhi and Haryana, Chitpavan of Maharashtra, and Goa, Anavala/Anavil of Gujarat, Nambuthiri of Kerala and Mohayal of Punjab and J&K. To trace out the origin, nature and hierarchial position of different castes, sub-castes and their position among various castes, the views of Manu's is given below in the following paragraphs.

"Manu represents, indeed, all the castes of Hindu society, and their number is considerable, as the result of mixed marriages between the four original castes. According to him the four primitive castes by intermarrying in every possible way gave rise to sixteen mixed castes, which by continuing their intermarriages produced the long list of the mixed castes. It is extremely doubtful, however, whether Manu meant to say that at all times the offspring of a mixed marriage had to enter a lower caste. He could not possibly maintain that the sons of a Brahman father and a Vaisya mother would always be a physician or Vaidya, this being the name given by Manu to the offspring of these two castes. At present the offspring of a Sudra father and a Brahman mother would find no admission in any respectable caste. Their marriage would not be considered marriage at all. The only rational explanation of Manu's words seems to be that originally the Vaidyas or physicians sprang from the union of a Brahman father and a Vaisya mother, though this, too, is of course nothing but a fanciful theory. If we look more carefully we shall find that most of these mixed castes are in reality the professions, trades and guilds of a half-civilised society. They did not wait for mixed marriages before they came into existence. Professions, trades and handicrafts had grown up without any reference to caste in the ethnological or political sense of the word. Some of their names were derived from towns and countries where certain professions were held in particular estimation. Servants who waited on ladies were called Vaidehas, because they came from Videha, the Athens of India, just as the Erench call the "porteur d'eau" a "Savoyard." To maintain that every member of the caste of the Vaidehas, in fact, every lady's maid, had to be begotten through the marriage of a Vaisya and a Brahmani, is simply absurd. In other cases the names of Manu's castes were derived from their occupations. The caste of musicians, for instance, were called Venas from *vina*, the lyre. Now, it was evidently Manu's object to bring these professional corporations in connection with the old system of castes, assigning to each, according to its higher or lower position, a more or less pure descent from the original castes. The Vaidyas, for instance, or the physicians, evidently a respectable corporation, were represented as the offspring of a Brahman father and a Vaisya mother, while the guild of the fishermen, or Nishadas, were put down as the descendants of a Brahman father and a Sudra mother. Manu could hardly mean to say that every son of a Vaisya father and Kshatriya mother was obliged to become a commercial traveller, or to enter the caste of Magadhas. How could that caste have been supplied after the extinction in many places of the Kshatriya and Vaisya castes? But having to assign to the Magadhas a certain social position, Manu recognised them as the descendants of the second and third castes, in the same way as the Herald's office would settle the number of quarters of an earl or a baron."

Before leaving the consideration of caste as found in Manu's "Institutes," It may be noted that we find side by side two discrepant views as to the connubium of the orders. According to the milder, and apparently the older view, caste is determined by descent from the father, and a Dvija or twice-born man may take a wife from among Brahmans, Kshatriyas or Vaisyas. With a Sudra woman alone he could not intermarry. By the other view a man was advised to marry a virgin of his own caste as his first wife, and after that he may proceed according to the rank of the castes. There is some reason to believe that under this rule he might take even a Sudra woman as a second wife. This, it is needless to say, represents a very different state of things from that which prevails under the modern rigid law of caste endogamy.

It was caste in or about the stage of its development exhibited in the "Institutes" of Manu which Megasthenes, first of all the Barbarians, observed in his embassy to the court of Sandrocottus or Chandragupta (306—298 B.C.). He found seven, not four, castes — the philosophers, husband-men, shepherds, artisans, soldiers, inspectors and counsellors of the king. The philosophers were the Brahmans, and the traveller indicates the prescribed stages of the Brahmanical life. He distinguishes the Brahmans from the Sarmanai, the latter of whom are supposed to represent the Buddhist Saramanas or Monks, while the inspectors were the Buddhist supervisors of morals, afterwards referred to in the sixth edict of Asoka.

The historical development of caste sufficiently disposes of the popular theory that caste is a permanent institution, transmitted unchanged from the dawn of Hindu history and myth.

Another and even graver misconception is to suppose that caste is peculiar to Hinduism and connected in some peculiarly intimate way with the Hindu faith. It is needless to say that caste as an institution is not confined to Indian soil. The Zendavasta shows that the early persian community was divided into three castes or tribes, of which one lived by hunting, a second by grazing flocks, and the third by agriculture. "In this respect also," says Herodotus, "the Lacedaemonians resemble the Egyptians : their heralds, musicians and cooks succeed to their fathers' professions : so that a musician is son to a musician, a cook, of a cook, and a herald, of a herald : nor do others, on account of the clearness of their voice, apply themselves to this profession and exclude others; but they continue to practise it after their fathers." This occupational or hereditary guild system of caste, which, as will be seen, was the most important factor in the development of this institution, prevailed and still prevails, as a matter of fact, all the world over. Nor is caste confined to votaries of the Hindu faith. On the contray it is in its nature much more social than religious. It has been one of the most perplexing problems which beset the Christian Missionary to reconcile the restrictions of caste with the perfect liberty of Christianity. Islam has boldly solved the difficulty by recognising and adopting caste in its entirety. Not only does the coverted Rajput, Gujar or Jat remain a member of his original sept or section; but they preserves most of those restrictions on social intercourse, intermarriage and the like, which make up the peasant's conception of caste. As Mr. Ibbetson remarks,— "Almost the only difference which the convert makes is to shave his scalplock and the upper edge of his moustache, to repeat the

Muhammadan creed in a mosque, and to add the Muhammadan to the Hindu marriage ceremony. As far a religion goes he worships Khuda instead of *Parameswar*, keeps up his service in honor of Bhawani, and regularly makes the due oblation for the repose of the sainted dead." On the other hand, as will be seen everywhere, the members of orthodox Hindu castes worship the quintette of the Panch Pir, or famous local saints like Miyan or Miran Sahib, Shah Madar or Sakhi Sarwar.

By another popular theory caste is eternal and immutable. The ordinary Hindu will say that it has always existed, that it is based on what he calls the Shastras, a vague body of religious literature of which he knows little more than the name. It has already been shown that the vague reference to caste in the Vedas discloses the institution at a very different stage from what we see it in the "Institutes" of Manu or at the present day. Even in an age so comparatively recent as that of Manu, the rules of connubium and social life were very different from those which prevail at present. The modern Vaishnava, for instance, would shudder at the comparatively liberal permission given in these days for the use of meat. But in addition to this we meet all through the range of Hindu history and myth with numerous illustrations of the mutability of caste. Thus in the Mahabharata, Bhima is married by his brother Yudhishthira to the Asura woman Hidimba, and the marriage rites are regularly performed; while Draupadi, a Kshatriya girl, accepts as her husband at the Swayamvara Arjuna who pretends to be a Brahman. Viswamitra, a Kshatriya by birth, compelled Brahma by the force of his austerities to admit him to the Brahmanical order, so that he might be on a level with Vasishtha, with whom he had quarrelled. It is even more significant to learn from the Mahabharata that all castes become

Brahmans when they have crossed the Gomati on a visit to the hermitage of Vasishtha, and that the country of the five rivers is contemptible because there is a Bahika or Panjabi "born a Brahman becomes afterwards a Kshatriya, a Vaisya or a Sudra, and eventually a barber."

Burnell has fixed the period of mixed caste origin, which began to take place in larger number during 500 AD and other historians are of the view that during 7th century AD, a large number of offspring came up due to intermarriages between Aryan and non-Aryans.

As regards the castes of the present day the case is similar. Instead of castes being a clearly-defined entity, an association complete in themselves, a trade guild the doors of which are rigidly barred against the admission of strangers, they are in a constant state of flux and flow. New endogamous groups are constantly being created, the process of fission is ever in operation, and what is more important still the *novus homo*, like his brethren all the world over, is constantly endeavouring to force his way into a higher grade and acquire the privileges of the "twice-born." This process is specially observable among the Gonds and other Dravidian races of the Central India. Thus the Raj Gonds who "in appearance obstinately retain the Turanian type, in aspiration are Hindus of the Hindus, wearing the sacred cord and carrying ceremonial refinements to the highest pitch of parvenu purism. Mr. Hislop says that not content with purifying themselves, their houses, and their food, they must even sprinkle their faggots with water before using them for cooking. With all this exterior coating of the fashionable faith they seem, however, to retain an ineradicable taint of the old mountain superstitions. Some of these outwardly Brahmanised chiefs still try to pacify the gods of their fathers for their apparent desertion of them by worshipping them in secret once every four or five years and by placing cow's flesh to their lips, wrapped in a cloth, so as not to break to openly with the reigning Hindu divinities." Captain Forsyth writes :— "In Gondwana numberous chiefs claim either a pure descent from Rajput houses, or more frequently admit their remote origin to have sprung from a union between some Rajput adventurer of noble blood and one of the daughters of the aborigines. Few of them are admitted to be pure Rajputs by the blue blooded chiefs of Rajasthan: but all have their bards and genealogies."

The same process of elevation of the aboriginal races have been going on for centuries throughout Northern India. To quote Mr. Nesfield :— "Local traditions in Oudh and the North-Western Provinces abound in tales of Brahmans being manufactured out of low caste men by Rajas when they could not find a sufficient number of hereditary Brahmans to attend some sacrifice or feast. For example, the Kunda Brahmans of Partabgarh are said to have been manufactured by Raja Manik Chand, because he was not able to collect the quorum of one hundred and twenty-five thousand Brahmans to whom he had vowed to make a feast : in this way an Ahir, a Kurmi or a Bhat found himself dubbed a Brahman and invested with the sacred thread, and their descendants are Brahmans to this day. A similar tale is told of Tirgunait Brahmans and Pathaks of Amtara: of the Pande Parivars in the Hardoi District: of the large clan called Sawalakhiyas in the Gorakhpur and Basti Districts, who have nevertheless assumed the high-sounding titles of Dube, Upadhya, Tiwari, Misra, Dikshit, Pande, Awasthi and Pathak. Only about a century and-a-half ago a Luniya, or man of the salt-making class, which ranks decidely low, was made a

Brahman by Raja Bhagwant Rae of Asothar, and this man is the ancestor of the Misra Brahmans of Aijhi."

The Bhumihars and Tagas, if they are really of genuine Brahmanical descent, have in the same way differentiated themselves by function, and having abandoned priestly duties are agriculturist and landowners pure and simple. This separation of function must have prevailed from very early times, because it was specially laid down that each caste may adopt the occupation of another in case of distress, and thus a Brahman may do the work of a Khestriya or Vaisya but not of a Sudra.

Similarly Bhumihar Brahman were carved out of necessities as other castes originated. Bhumihar Brahman/Bhabhan has always been a large and influential caste in undivided Bihar. They have Brahmanical gotras, titles and family names as also similar customs. They use the Brahmanical titles and surnames of Misra, Pandey, Tiwari alongwith the Rajput ones of Rai, Singh, Thakur. Other titles such as Mahto, Sinha, Parashar, Chaudhary, Prasad, Mowar etc; are also used by the Bhumihars of Bihar. They perform half the rites prescribed for a Brahman. In Shahabad, and other parts they were accorded Pranam (greetings) usually reserved for Brahmans, but further south this Practice was unknown. In Shahabad it was the Babhan who gave the first greeting to the Kayastha. There position varied in different parts of the state. In south-east Bihar, they ranked immediately below the Kayasthas but in Shahabad and Saran (Siwan, Chapra etc.) they were on the same level as the Rajputs. There sectional names appears to be of two types: territorial referring either to some very early settlement of the section or to the birth-place of its founder, and eponymous, the eponym being in most cases a vedic rishi. The names and forms of clans correspond with or were closely related to those current among the Rajputs but some names were Brahmanical. They are chiefly cultivators by occupation, a profession usually looked upon as being beneath the dignity of a Brahman. A great majority of them are Zamindars and have assumed secular titles of Raja and Maharaja like the Rajputs.

This caste is spread all over the state but in certain pockets of the state it is concentrated. In the South Gangetic Plain from the Barabar Hills, to the Rajgir-Jethian Hills and the Kharakpur Hills and in these hills lies the districts of Gaya, Patna and Monghyr forming a number of seperate ridges or isolated peaks which strike north-eastward until they reach the Ganga in the Kharakpur hills, near the town of Monghyr. Bhumihar Brahmans are spread over in these areas of the state. The Kaimur hills, seperated from the rest of the Plateau by the valley of the son also houses this caste. The Ganga which is joined by Ghaghra from the North (12 mils north of Arrah), by the Son from the South near Bihta and by the Gandak opposite Patna. Construction of bridge over Ganga has also reduced the distance from Patna to Muzaffarpur (a Bhumihar dominated area) and rail-road bridge on the Ganga at Mokameh Ghat has made easy to move this caste easly to another caste fellow on occasions. The maximum of rainfall is attributed in the above areas of the state barring a few districts outside.

Magadh with its own unique history and the earliest ruling dynasty founded by Brihadratha was the centre core of Bihar in the ancient period. It consists of modern districts of Patna, Jehanabad, Gaya, Arrah, Sasaram, Punpun, Fathua, Monghyr, (Begusarai, Barahia), Bhagalpur and some recently created districts. At present heavy concentration of this caste is found in most of these districts. Buchanan has called Bhumihars as Magadh Brahmin. Density of population in these areas are also very high, as for example, Patna district has density of 912, Bhojpur - 904, Jehanabad - 920, Gaya - 924, Saran - 967, Muzzafarpur -906, Begusarai - 898, Monghyr - 884, Khagaria - 868 etc.; (per 1000 males, 1991 census). Similarly physiological density is also high in these areas (It is an expression of population presure differentially exerted on agricultural land). Sex ratio of these districts are low, as for Patna it is 868, Munghyr (884) Khagaria (868) etc.; only in some other districts this ratio is comparatively high, which indicate the preference of this caste in favour of male child against female as a whole.

Though Bihar is an integral part of the hindi speaking region of India and it is the state language, but not the mother tongue of all people of the State. Maithili, Magadhi and Bhojpuri languages are used by this caste accordingly. (areas in which they resides). Magadhi is spoken in the districts of Patna, Gaya, Jehanabad, and in most of the newly created districts from old Patna districts. Similarly, Bhojpuri is spoken in districts like Arrah, Buxur, Chapra. Siwan, Sasaram etc.; and Gorakhpur and Banaras divisions of U.P.; Maithili with its slightest versions are spoken in parts of Muzaffarpur, Bhagalpur, Apbhransha or as Dr. Grierson has termed 'Bihari' as mixture of speeches of the above three languages are spoken in other parts of the state here and there. So, no specific language is used by this caste but mostly they speak 'Bihari' mentioned above.

During struggle for independence this caste played a pivotal role and people like late Sh. S.K. Sinha occupied important position in the state politics and in the field of spreading education. One cannot forget the contribution of Sir Ganesh Dutt besides Swami Sahajanand in the field of creating awareness through education.

Once Dhoti, Kurta and Banddi was the main dress for men and sari for women of this caste but now a days influence of western fashion can be seen in their dress pattern. Similarly now they have begin to experiment with different food items but in villages staple diet even today's is rice, wheat and vegetables. Frequently they also used cereals (dal).

The documentry sources includes some case studies, books, journals, census reports and other publications related to this caste.

In addition to this, help of important persons belonging to this caste, their memoirs and Brahmarshi Samaj Patrika published from Kankerbagh, Patna etc., were taken during field investigations.

References

- Buhler : Sacred laws of the Aryans 1,209, 211, 11, 12.
- *Institutes*, III., 12—15: 44 : IX., 22, 24; 85—87 : III., 16—19: X., 5, 6; 10—15 : with Duneker's comments, *History of Antiquity*, IV., 245 p.
- *Institutes* V., 22 *sq*.
- Wilson, *Rig Veda*, II., 319.
- *Vishnu Purana*, *Book* IV., Cap. J., p. 359 : Cap. XIX., p. 451 : Muir, *Ancient Sanskrit Texts*, I., 222 *sqq*., 227; 238; 426 *sqq*. Wilson, *Rig Veda*, I., 42 note : Essays, II., 309 : Max Muller, *Chips from a German Workshop*, II., 339 *sq*. *Ancient Sanskrit Literature*, 58 *sq*., and compare Rajendra
- Grant, *Introduction, Central Provinces Gazetter*, CX., *sq*.

2

Origin of the Caste

Our understanding of caste as a system of inequality is derived from (i) Indological sources, from the Hindu sacred literature and other literatures available on castes and (ii) from census reports, gazetteers and ethnographic glossaries as well as accounts based on intensive field work.

Caste is a Portuguese word meaning clan. The earliest reference to caste occurs in the Rigveda (2nd Millennium B.C.), which states four category of castes, i.e., Brahmin, Kshatriya, Vaishya and Sudra. Later on to adjust many other sub-castes due to development in this field, Brahminical community (including Manu Smriti) supplemented these with different dharmas and the Jati dharma, that is, the *dharma* to be followed by each sub-castes or grouping within the four walls of caste system emerged. So Caste is also viewed in Varna term.

Dumont's in his "Homo Hierarchicus" explained the caste theory on the basis of principle of purity and pollution (closed endogamous descent groups). It shows that the Varna Hierarchy was in his mind with Brahman at the top of the ladder.

While following the intellectual lead of Hutton (1946), Leach mentions, as below, the minimal set of primary characteristics, which together embody the real essence of caste everywhere: (i) A caste is endogamous, (2) There is a hierarchical grading of castes, the best-recognised position being that of the Brahmin at the top, (3) There are restrictions on commensality between members of different castes, (4) In various kinds of contact, especially those concerned with food, sex, and ritual, a member of high caste is liable to be polluted by a member of low caste (5) Castes are very commonly associated with traditional occupations, (6) A man's caste status is firmly determined by the circumstances of his birth unless he comes to be expelled from his caste for some ritual offence, (7) The system, as a whole, is always focused around the prestige accorded to the Brahmins (Leach, Ed., 1962 : 2)

Ghurye emphasises on six out-standing features of Hindu caste society. (1) Segmental division of society, (2) hierarchy (3) restrictions on feeding and social intercourse, (4) Civil and religious dis-abilities and privileges on different sections (5) lack of unrestricted choice of occupations and (6) restrictions on marriage (1969). Bougle (1971) stresses on the hierarchy, hereditary occupational specialization and mutual repulsion, as the three cardinal features of caste. According to Risley, "A caste may be defined as a collection of families, or groups of families bearing a common name which usually denotes or is associated with specific occupation claiming common descent from a mythical ancestor, human or divine, professing to follow the same callings and are regarded by those who are competent to give an opinion as forming a single homogenous community. Ketkar own definition of caste recognizes it as a social group and brings into relief characteristics such as birth ascription. endogamy, exclusiveness, hierarchy, pretensions to purity of blood etc.; (1979). According to Gough, "castes in Hindu India are ranked as birth-status group. The caste system of the Hindus of India is considered as an archetype by comparative sociologists. Although a double usage of the concept of caste is concurrent, recognizing it both as an "ethnographic category" and as a "sociological category" (Leach, Ed, 1962). The Bhumihar Brahmin/Babhan situation is analysed using the ethnographic Hindu meaning for obvious reasons.

Before going into the origin of the Bhumihar caste, it would be appropriate to know the tentative position (not exact) of this caste among the fourfold varnas as described in the Hindu shastra.

From the previous chapter, we came to know about the "mixed castes" or sub castes, i.e.; offspring from the main four castes (Manu's description) due to intermarriages or as "Nesfield" has classified it on the basis of occupation, such as (i) Casteless tribes, (ii) Castes allied to the hunting stage, (iii) Castes allied to the fishing stage, (iv) Caste allied to the pastoral stage, followed by (v) Landlord and Warrior, (vi) Agriculturist and dominant caste, (vii) Serving castes. Taga/Tyagi and Bhumihar belongs to agricultur.st and dominant warrior caste, as is shown in the table below:

Table
Classification of caste by traditional occupation

Class	Caste or Tribe	Strength
Military and dominant Caste	Bhumihar	221,031
	Jat	698,826
	Rajput	3,633,843
	Taga/Tyagi	128,563

Most of the so-called "mixed castes" owe their exclusiveness to either Brahmincal policy, or to the impossibility of including them within any of the four primary groups. What seems much more probable is, that in order to make the primary divisions into four castes practically acceptable, most of the sub-divisions in each of them had to be recognised at the very beginning, and the tendency which was thus generated received further expansion by the recognition of the additional castes on account of the prevailing circumstances, and in this process Bhumihars came in picture. Previously they were known as 'Babhans' which was somewhat inferior in hearing. So efforts by Swami Sahajanand Saraswati was made in this direction to call this caste by Bhumihar Brahman. For this he putforth examples from Hindu shastra and proved that 'Babhans' are Brahmans (Bhumihar) and is not inferior in any way to the Brahman (priest).

So keeping in view the accepted norms and higher social status provided to this caste in the present scenario because it follows all the Brahmnical rituals, rules etc., with minor differences and so in 1931 Census it was put just below the Brahman in hierarchy.

The literal meaning of Bhumihar is Bhumi — "Land", Kara or Hara-"Maker" in sanskrit. In the language of the Indian feudal system, Bhum is the name given to a kind of tenure similar to the Inams and Jagirs of Mohammedan times. By a Bhum, according to the Rajputana Gazetteer, an hereditary non-resumable and inalienable property in the soil was inseparably bound up with a revenue - free title. Bhum was given as compensation for bloodshed in order to quell a feud for distinguished sevices in the field, for protection of services in the field, for protection of a border, or for the watch and ward of a village. The meaning of the designation Bhumihar being as stated above, the Bhumihar Brahmans are evidently those Brahmans who held grants of land for secular services. Whoever held a secular fief was a Bhumihar. Where a Brahman held such a tenure he was called a Bhumihar Brahman. Where the holder was a Kshatriya, he was called a Bhumihar Kshatriya. Bhumihar Brahmans are sometimes called simply Bhumihars. It is an important caste of landowners and agriculturists in the eastern part of the country, i.e.; in undivided Bihar, in U.P. this caste was migrated from Tekari in Bihar and distributed in the eastern districts of the state; and in some parts of Bengal. Some of the big landholders of this caste who were called Rajas are given below :

1. Raja of Benaras
2. Raja of Bethia in Champaran, (North Bihar)
3. Raja of Tekari in Gaya
4. Raja of Hathwa in Saran (Siwan), North Bihar.
5. Raja of Tamakhi in Gorakhpur.
6. Raja of Sheohar.
7. Raja of Maisadal in Midnapur, West Bengal
8. Raja of Pakour in Santhal Pargana (Jharkhand)
9. Raja of Maheshpur in Santhal Pargana (Jharkhand)

In Assam the Bhumihar hold their lands on very favourable terms but no exceptional indulgence is shown in respect of Bhumihars of Bihar or U.P. by the local Zamindars. As may be expected the Bhumihar, a chiefly agricultural class, they never touched the plough in the past. Bhumihar are also known as Babhan, Zamindar Brahman, Grihastha Brahman or Pachhima Brahman (H.H. Risley).

Bhumihar Brahman is of a relatively recent nomenclature. It emerged during the latter half of the nineteenth century when the Babhan made representation to claim their identity as Bhumihar Brahman. As Babhan is a Pali word, the language prevailent during Buddha period (6th Century B.C.). Some peoples associate Chanakya with Bhumihar, which clearly indicate that this caste exist during the period. The Bhumihar Mahasabha, which had been active since 1896, represented their claim for recognition and in the 1931 census they were placed below the Brahman in the Bihar list of castes. Behind the clubbing of the Bhumihar with the Brahman in the 1931 census lay the movement of social mobility by which they sought the upgrading of their status to that of the Brahman's. Swami Sahajanand Saraswati included the Bhumihar in the category of the non-begging (ayachak) Brahman, who being landowners had lost touch with Brahmanical rituals and the knowledge of sanskrit. The Tyagi, etc.; are also included in this category of Ayachak Brahman.

Regarding the origin of the Babhans, a variety of traditions are current. One story represents them as the descendants of the Brahman rulers whom Parsuram set up in the place of the Kshatriya slain by him and who in course of time abandoned their Brahmanical duties and took to the profession of land holding. Another tells how a certain King of Ayodhya being childless, sought to remove his reproach by the sacrifice of a Brahman, and bought for this purpose the second son of the Rishi Jamadagni, the father of Parsuram. By the intervention of Vishwamitra, the maternal uncle of the victim, the Raja was enabled to get a child without bloodshed, but the young Brahman was held to have been degraded by the sale, and was called upon to settle down on the land and become the forefather of the Babhan caste. The legend refered to is that of Sunah Sephas, told in the Aitareya Brahman and in a slightly different form in the Ramayan. A third legend perhaps the best known of all traces the Babhan back to a sacrifice offered by Jarasandha, King of Magadha, at which a very large number of Brahman some say a lakh and a quarter were required to be present. Jarasandha's Dewan, a Kayastha of the Amasht or Karan sub-caste, did his best to meet the demand but was driven to eke out the local supply by distributing sacred threads among members of the lower castes and palming them off on the king as genuine Brahmans. Jarasandha's suspicious being roused by the old appearance of some of the guests, the Dewan was compelled to guarantee their respectability by eating the food which they had cooked; while the Brahmans thus manufactured, failing to gain addmission into their supposed caste, had to set up a caste of their own, the name of which (Babhan or Brahman) is popularly supposed to mean a Sham Brahman, "Just as in some districts an inferior Rajput is called a Raut the corruption of the name betokening the corruption of the caste."

The last theory is at once refuted by the appearance and demeanour of the caste. They are, "according to Mr. Beames." a fine manly race, with the delicate Aryan type of feature in full perfection". This type is singularly uniform and persistent among the Babhans, which would not be the case if they were descended from a crowd of low-caste men promoted by the exigencies of a particular occasion, for brevet rank thus acquired would in no case carry with it the right of inter-marriage with pure Brahmans or Rajputs and the artificially formed group, being compelled to marry within its own limits, would necessarily perpetuate the low caste type of feature and complexion. As a matter of fact, this is what happens with the sham Rajputs whom in most of the outlying districts of Bengal. They marry among themselves, never among the true Rajput and their features reproduce those of the particular aboriginal tribe (caste) from which they may happen to have sprung.

The next supposition is that they may be Brahmans who for some cause have been degraded.

There are, of course, many so-called Brahman like the Mahabrahmans, Ojha or Dakaut, who are of a degraded type; but many of these are almost certainly derived from the lower races and have little or no Aryan blood in their veins. Further, many true Brahman hold land and cultivate, and are not necessarily degraded by doing so.

An examination of the sections or exogamous groups into which the Babhans are divided appears, however, strongly against the hypothesis that they are degraded Brahmans. These groups are usually the oldest and most durable element in the internal organization of a caste and may therefore be expected to offer the clearest indications as to its origin.

Brahmans do not eat with them nor do Rajputs. Possibly the existence of the Bhumihar class is also evidence of the time when the bonds of caste had not been forged, or if forged, were not worn by those who pushed forward into new settlements beyond the old. It has been pointed out that to the non-Aryan inhabitants of the country all Aryans were of one caste, – all Brahmans. Within the Aryan body the exchange of priestly for military employment was not impossible and did not involve degradation. It is necessary, therefore, to believe that all Bhumihars are Brahmans of inferior rank because of illegitmate stock, according to mixed castes theory discussed earlier but many of the caste fellow donot believe in this theory. They may be as true born as the Brahmans or Kshetriyas who surround them, and many of whom they possible preceded in the occupation of the land.

Dr. Oldham, speaking of the Ghazipur branch of Bhumihar says that in popular estimation they share something of the sacredness which attaches to Brahmans.

Their divisions are very often the same as those

of well known Rajputs, such as the Kinwar, Gautam and the Kausik Bhumihars. In one case "a Bhumihar and a Rajput caste both claim descent from a common ancestor, and each admits that the pretensions of the others are well founded. The Bhumihar caste all intermarry on terms of equality and eat together; on the other hand Rajputs marry their daughters into what they consider superior and their sons into inferior castes and are very chary of eating together. There is consequently a much closer bond of sympathy between the various Bhumihar castes of the districts than between the Rajputs."

Sir H.M. Elliot was of the view that "we perhaps have some indication of the true origin of the Bhumihars in the names of Garga Bhumi and Vasta Bhumi, who are mentioned in the Harivansa as Kshetriya Brahmans, descendents of Kasya princes." Their name of Bhumi and residence of Kashi are much in favour of this view; moreover, there are to this day Garga and Vatsa Gotras among the Sarwariya Brahmans."

We also find among the Babhan section-names of two distinct types : —the one territorial referring either to some very early settlement of the section, or to the birth place of its founder, and the other eponymous, the eponym being in most cases a Vedic Rishi or inspired saint. The names of the former class correspond to or closely resemble those current among Rajputs; the names of the latter are those of the standard Brahmanical gotras. When the matrimonial prohibitions based on these two classes of section conflict, as must obviously often happen where every member of the caste necessarily belongs to both sets, the authority of the territorial class over-rides that of the eponymous or Brahmanical class. Suppose, for instance, that a man of the Karranch territorial section and of the Sandilya eponymous section wishes to marry a woman of the Sakarwar territorial section, the fact that she also belongs to the Sandilya eponymous section will not operate as a bar to the marriage. Whatever may be the theory of the purohit of the caste, the Brahmanical gotra is disregarded in practice, and doubtful cases are decided in accordance with the mul or territorial section to which the parties belong. This indicate the importance of territorial section and probably the original sections of the caste. If Babhan had originally been Brahmans they would at the time of their seperation from the parent caste have been already filled up with a complete set of Brahmanical gotras, and it is difficult to imagine any reason which could have induced them to borrow a strange and much more elaborate set of sections from a caste of inferior status and to relegate their own sections to an entirely subordinate position. Territorial sections, moreover, donot lend themselves to the process of borrowing. They are as a rule exceedingly numerous; the meanings of their names are obscure and difficult to trace; and, with the exception of a few names borne by famous Rajput clan, they are wanting in the note of social distinction. The Brahmanical gotras, on the other hand, form a clearly defined and not inconveniently-numerous group to which well known and honourable traditions attach, and the influence of Brahman purohits is sufficient to diffuse them throughout any caste which affect a high standard of ceremonial purity and wishes to rise in the social scale.

Mr. Sherring lays stress on the fact that the Bhumihar of Benaras call themselves Brahmans; have the gotras, titles, and family names of Brahmans and practice for the most part the usages of Brahmans". In Bihar though their claim to be Brahmans is not invariably put forward, Brahmanical titles such as Mishra, Pandey and Tewari are used along with the Rajput titles of Singh, Rai and Thakur.

The question then of the origin of the Bhumihars is not capable of exact determination. Their traditions, customs and appearance point all to a Brahmanical origin; their caste organisation seems to show that they are not as is asserted by some, Brahmans who for a reason obviously-inadequate, have been degraded from their original position. They may be a real branch of the Aryan stock, who in very remote ages colonised the part of the country which they occupy at present and being reduced by the exigencies of their position to abrogate their sacerdotal functions, took to a life of war and agriculture and in consequence of this organised their caste in a manner analogous to those of the early Kshetriya settlers.

Caste Organisation

The Bhumihars are organised on both the territorial and eponymous systems. Of the former the chief sub-divisions in the eastern part of these provinces are the Kinwaar, Donwaar, Sakarwar, Baghochhiya Bemuwaar, Karenawa, Kotraha, Karmai, Kolhaniyaan, Athariya, Jaithariya, Chaudhari, Kotaha, Sobraniyan, Belhariya Domkatar, Baksariya, Eksariya, Gautamiya, Titiha, Bhaiwadh, Kolaha, Sorhaniya, Biruar, Surohan, Birramiya, Kahatwar, Mirzapuri, Raikwar, and Parasiya. Besides these there are a number of sub-divisions of the Brahmanical type such as Dikshit Garga, Gautam, Sandilya, Pande, Dubey, Tewari, Upadhaya, Pathak, Shukla, Kapilgotri, Kausik, Bhardwaja, and Payasi Mishra, They further enumerate eightyfour types of the regular Brahmanical gotras, such as Kashyapa, Vasishta, Parasara, Bhargava, Vatsya, Katyayana, Gargya, Gobhila, Angiras and so on. But in carrying out the rules of exogamy the mul or territorial section is alone taken account of, and not the Brahmanical gotra. With this exception the prohibited degrees follow the standard

Brahmanical formula. Some of these sections are possibly to temistic such as, the Baghochhiya Belauria, Kastuar or Tiger (Baagh), Domkatar — Dom's Knife, Belhariya from the bel tree, Hararia – "foundling", Kodaria – "spade-wielder," Bhusbarat – "husk-picker" and these sections carry with them some degree of inferiority, which results in a form of hypergamy. The census returns give no less than 485 Bhumihar sections; but here the territorial sections and the Brahmanical gotras are mixed up together. The most important local sections according to these returns are the Chaudhary, Gautam and Kolaha in Benaras, the Gautam in Mirzapur, the Bhardwaja, Bhrigubansi, Dixit, Donwar, Gautam, Kaushik Kinwar, Kistwar, Sakarwar, Sonwar, in Ghazipur, the Asuriya, Bhagata, Domkatar, Kinwar, Manchaura, Nanauliya and Bemwar of Ballia, the Baghochhiya, Baksariya, Gautam, Kaushik and Sakarwar of Gorakhpur; the Barasi, Birhariya and Kaushik of Basti, and the Barwar, Bhardwaja Bhrigubans, Denwar, Gargbans, Gautam, Purwar, Sakarwar and Sandil of Azamgarh.

Territorial Sub-divisions: Among the higher castes territorial names for exogamous sections or septs are curiously mixed up with names preserving the memory of a chief who founded or led the sept within historic time and with the mythical eponyms of the Brahmans, Babhans etc.; of Bihar both of whom prohibits marriage within the section of either father or mother. There is differentiation at the territorial levels (Rai, Singh, Bhokta) among the Bhumihar. All the sub groups are linked with one another in superior subordinate relationships.

Some accounts of the chief territorial sub-divisions are given here:

a) ***Kinwar Bhumihar*** : It claimed its origin from Padampur in the carnatic, like the Kinwar

Rajputs. They have in Ghazipur three sub-sections – Rajdhar, Makund and Pithaur Rae.

b) ***Bemwar*** : The Bemwar Bhumihars came from Bempur and settled in Narwan in Benaras. They are respectable, well-to-do People.

c) ***Sakarwar*** : The Sakarwar Bhumihars are closely connected with the Rajput sept of the same name, and like them their legends connect them and their name with Fatehpur-Sikri. In Ghazipur they are generally rich and have retained the greater part of their ancestral property.

d) ***Donwar*** : The Donwar sub-division say that their original home was near Fatehpur-Sikri. When they settled in Azamgarh they were known as Bhath. They derive their name from the parent village Donauli, which took its name from Dona Acharya, a Panre Brahman. Dr. Oldham says that they are frugal and industrious. The ancestor of the Donwars of two or three villages was in the millitary service of one of the Delhi emperors and received from him for his valour the title of Khan, which is borne to the present day by all his descendants.

e) ***Gautam*** : Tradition runs that about the year 304 Hijri (882 A.D.), a Brahman of the Gautam Gotra named Khattu Mishra came to Benaras. Every day after he had bathed he used to pour some water at the root of a madar tree (Asclepias gigantea) in which lived a Rakshasha. One day he forgot to make the accustomed offering and the Rakshasha appeared and request him to relieve his thirst. He complied with the request and the Rakshasa offered him any boon he choses. Khattu replied that he was much inconvenienced by having to dry his wet loin over his shoulders whenever he went to bathe. So the demon gave him the power of throwing the cloth into the air, where it was miraculously suspended until it dried. The Rakshasa then introduced him to Vyasa, who was living in Benaras and the fame of his miracles rapidly brought him reputation and wealth. So, he built a tank at Benaras, which is still known as *Mishra Ka Pokhara* and planted trees on its bank. Benaras was then ruled by Raja Banar and one day an elephant belonging to the Raja injured one of the trees of Khattu Mishra, where at he was wroth, and the Raja was forced to take the worthy into his favour. One day the Raja gave Khattu a packet of betel on which he had written a deed-of-gift of twenty eight villages. Khattu unwittingly swallowed the betel and being considered to have thus lost status by accepting a gift, he henceforth lost the power of drying his loin cloth in the air. This estate was the present Gangapur, which belongs to his descendant the present Maharaja of Benaras, who belongs to the Bipra branch of the Gautam gotra, with the title of Mishra. According to Mr Sherring it is "of the Kauthumiya Sakha, or branch of Brahman following the ritual of the Sama Veda. It has three Pravaras, distinguished by the number of Knots in the Brahmamical cord - the Gautam, Angiras, and Anthatiya. The clan inter-marries with the Bhumihars of the Madhyandina Sakha of Brahmans observing the ritual of the Yajur-veda. It is traditionally allied to the Sarwariya Brahmans of Madhubani beyond the Ghaghra.

f) ***Maneria*** : During Mughal period due to certain circumstances which compelled the Bhumihars of Maner area to leave the place and settle in other areas such as Bihta, Datiyana and other adjoining villages in Patna district of Bihar state and thus derived its name as Maneria Babhan/Bhumihar.

g) ***Hararia, Kodaria, Bhusbarat, Domkatar*** : The nick names seem to be of same kind as we meet among some of the himalayan castes. In the absence of evidence that the members of the first three sections regard with veneration the animal and plants whose name they bear. It is hardly justified in pronouncing the names to be suvivals from the totemistic stage. Some suggestions of inferiority does, however, seems to attach to these territorial sections.

h) ***Jujhotia Brahman*** : They got their name from one Jujhar Singh, a ruler of remote antiquity, who settled in Bundelkhand and finding no Brahmans they imported Kanaujias from the north side of the Jamuna and called them by this name. Not only do they thus assert Kanaujia origin but they incidently honour the present ruler of Charkhari whose name happens to be Jujhar Singh. Regarded as similar but inferior to Kanaujias whose Pakki they will eat though Kanaujias do not return the compliment. Vishnu Dharm Puran calls the country between the Vindhyas, Jamuna and Narbada, Yudhdesh and in this tract Jujhotias are chiefly found.

On their relationships to Brahmans and Rajputs a competent observer, Mr. J.R. Reid, writes : - Their Brahman and Chhatri neighbours generally insinuate that they are of mixed breed, the offspring of Brahman men and Chhatri women, or of Chhatri men and Brahman women. By other castes they are regarded as a kind of Chhatri, and are spoken of, and indeed often speak of themselves, as Bhumihar Thakurs. Their clans (gotra) are the same as those of the

Brahman, and, like the latter, the Bhumihars wear a thread (Janeu) ninety six hands breadth (Chaua) in length, the Chhatri's thread being eighty only. They donot perform priestly offices nor receive offerings given from a religious motive (daan dakshina); but they are saluated with the Pranam or Paelagi and return the salutation with a blessing (asirbad). Physically they are of the same type as the Brahman or Chhatri. In character they resemble the former more than the latter; and the following proverbs are in vogue :-

Nadi Kai bhawaoh,
Bhumihar Kai ghanwaoh,
Sabse Chatur Baniya, tese chatur Sunar;
Lase luse laike tehi thage Bhumihar.

"The Bhumihar is as uncertain as the current of the rivulet. Cutest of all is the Baniya; cutter than him is the Goldsmith; but the Bhumihar with his wiles tricks them both."

The total population of the (Babhan) Bhumihar in the country, according to the 1931 census, was 11, 13, 541, grouped under the cultivating Brahman but independent of the Brahman who were classified under the priestly category. They were returned mainly from Bihar and Orissa (895,602), United Provinces (19,08,50), Central Provinces and Berar (25,628), Bengal (847) and Central India (614). The Bhumihar were thus enumerated independently of the Brahman in the 1911, 1921 (as Babhan) and 1931 censuses. Their population in Bihar and Orissa declined from 11, 29, 735 in 1911 to 9,79,369 in 1921 and further to 8,95,602 in 1931.

According to W.G. Lacey, the localities in which the Babhan are most numerous are five out of the six districts of North Bihar (Purnea being excluded) and the four South Bihar districts. The following statement shows the actual number of Babhan and Brahmans emumerated in these nine districts in 1931 and compares the present position with that found a generation ago :-

In 1901 the Babhans in all these districts taken together outnumbered the Brahmans by some 85,500; later on the Brahmans had numerical superiority of 425,000. Assuming an equal rate of natural growth by both these communities there has been a transfer of more than 225,000 person from Babhans to Brahman in the course of the last thirty years, and one person out of every four who has returned as a Babhan in 1901 was then shown as Brahman. The process had been carried to an extreme length in the district of Darbhanga, where over a lakh of Babhans (or two out of every three in the district) had achieved this transformation. Bhagalpur, Monghyr and Shahbad came next in order but to a greater or less degree the same process has been going on in every district. During this last decade there had been no slackening in the tide of transfer of the nine district mentioned. Saran was the only one that donot show an actual decrease in the number of Babhans since 1921, and in Saran their rate of growth (4.0 percent) was well below the general rate. In Bhagalpur there had been a decrease of 10,500 or nearly 40.0 percent in the Babhan community. In Darbhanga the decrease was over 22,000 or 30.0 percent, in Monghyr 37,000 or over 20.0 percent, while in Muzaffarpur and Shahabad record decreases of about 13.0 percent each took place. There had, however, been a substantial increase in the number of Babhans in localities where they were less plentiful such as Hazaribagh, the Santhal Parganas, Purnea, Manbhum and Palamu.

Table

District	Babhans		Brahmans		Variation Percent (1901-31) in		
	1931	1901	1931	1901	TP	Babhans	Brahmans
Patna	106743	113655	58566	38849	+13.68	– 6.08	+ 50.75
Gaya	164731	163108	74297	64350	+15.84	+ 1.00	+ 15.46
Shahabad	61176	82334	199544	207071	+1.71	– 25.61	– 3.63
Saran	95422	106098	176875	184322	+3.21	– 10.06	– 4.04
Champaran	53161	52453	91941	84949	+19.84	+ 1.35	+ 8.23
Muzaffarpur	165446	200085	130927	99179	+6.71	– 17.31	+ 32.01
Darbhanga	49065	154345	321382	197967	+8.70	– 68.21	+ 62.34
Monghyr	138742	188959	113285	60353	+10.48	– 26.58	+ 87.70
Bhagalpur	16857	37973	109722	76532	+6.97	– 55.61	+ 43.37

Distribution of Bhumihar, according to the census of 1891 in present day U.P.

District	Number
Bulandshahr	1
Benaras	21,272
Mirzapur	9,385
Jaunpur	4,292
Ghazipur	54, 606
Balia	25,777
Gorakhpur	31,202
Basti	12,744
Azamgarh	61,425
Lucknow	86
Faizabad	124
Gonda	1
Pratapgarh	112
Total	221,027

According to 1931 Census, the proportion of elite cultivating castes in the population of Uttar Pradesh was as follows :

Table
Castes in Uttar Pradesh

Elite Cultivating Castes	Name of the castes	Percentage in total population
	Jats	1.6
	Bhumihars	0.4
	Tyagis	0.1
	Total	2.1

At the time of Akbar, in upper doab region, Jats, muslims, Tyagis and Gujaras held huge estates. In some of the districts of Uttar Pradesh, the caste composition of the revenue payers (as percentage of total revenue payers) at the time of Akbar was as follows:

Table

Castes	**Agra**	**Bulandshahar**	**Saharanpur**	**Jaunpur**
Rajputs	54.0	54.0	19.5	64
Brahmins	3.3	3.8	7.0	—
Jats	19.8	—	—	—
Muslims	5.1	—	—	11
Gujars	N.A.	11.6	7.9	—
Tyagis	—	3.0	27.0	—
Brahmin-Bhumihar	—	—	—	6
Brahman Rajput	—	—	—	18

Source : Trivedi, 1975 and Cohn, 1968

Table

The following statment shows the number and distribution of Babhans as ascertained in the census of 1872 and 1881- (then Calcutta Presidency)

District	**1872**	**1881**
Howrah	—	83
24 Parganas	—	14
Jessore	—	4
Murshidabad	—	160
Rajshahya	—	1
Rangpur	—	4
Patna	—	119

Contd...

Darjiling	—	11
Kuch Bihar	15	
Patna	116,714	121,495
Gaya	140, 244	152,697
Shahabad	72,038	76, 339
Tirtut [Darbhanga,	318,597	127,424
Muzaffarpur]		190,625
Saran	97,064	93,231
Champaran	49,288	52,415
Munger	160,973	176,958
Bhagalpur	39,764	42,358
Purnea	6,585	11,842
Santhal Parganas	102	6,089
Maldah	—	96
Hazaribagh	6,369	29,596
Lohardaga	5,786	11,648
Singhbhum	—	3
Tributarg States	—	13,250

Table

Bifurcation of data pertaining to Babhans (Bhumihar Brahman) is given below based on 1931 Census of India.

Caste and Districts	**Persons**	**Males**	**Females**
Babhan	895,602	472,639	422,963
Patna	106,743	58,503	48,240
Gaya	164,731	87,777	76,954
Shahabad	61,176	32,369	28,807
Saran	95,422	47,735	47,687
Champaram	53,161	27,563	25,598

Contd..

Muzaffarpur	165,446	83,728	81,718
Darbhanga	49,065	25,711	23,354
Monghyr	138,742	75,920	62,822
Bhagalpur	16,857	9,585	7,272
Purnea	3,693	2,203	1,490
Santhal Pargana	11,027	6,074	4,953
Hazaribagh	21,467	11,283	10,184
Palamu	2,503	1,270	1,233
Manbhum	4,624	2,466	2,158

After 1931, caste wise census enumeration was discontinued by the Government on certain grounds. So the authentic data (from Government, side) is not available after that. Only here and there some references had been made regarding this caste population, (12,50,647 projected data, 1971) so it has been left outside the purview of the study. Report on the Backward Classes Commission, 1st Part, vol. : I & II, 1980 has shown the percentage distribution of Indian population by caste and religious groups.

Table

S. No.	Group Name	Percentage of total population	
A.	I. Schedule Castes and Scheduled Tribes		
	Scheduled Castes	15.05	
	Scheduled Tribes	7.51	
	Total of 'A'	22.56	
B.	II. Non-Hindu Communities, Religious Groups, etc.		
	Muslims (other than STs)	11.9	(0.02)
	Christians (other than STs)	2.16	(0.44)
	Sikhs (other than SCs & STs)	1.67	(0.22)
	Budhists (other than STs)	0.67	(0.03)
	Jains	0.47	
	Total of 'B'	16.16	

C.	III. Foreward Hindu Castes & Communities	
	Brahmins (including Bhumihars)	5.52
	Rajputs	3.90
	Marathas	2.21
	Jats	1.00
	Vaishyas-Bania, etc.	1.88
	Kayasthas	1.07
	Other forward Hindu castes, groups	2.00
	Total of 'C'	17.58
	Total of 'A', 'B' & 'C'	56.30
	IV. Backward Hindu Castes & Communities	
D.	Remaining Hindu castes, groups which come in the category of "Other Backward Classes"	43.70
		100.00

Anthropometric Characteristics

The identification of the communities and their listing began at an early period of our history, with Manu. Regional lists of communities figured in sanskrit works. Medieval chronicals contained a description of communities located in various parts of the country. Listings in the colonial period were undertaken on an extensive scale after 1806. The process gathered momentum in course of the censuses from 1881 to 1941. Credit goes to A.S.I. for bringing out descriptive anthropological profile of all the communities of India, the impact on them of change and development processes and the links that bring them together.

The general population in the eastern region, comprising Bihar. (including Jharkhand), West Bengal, Orissa and some adjoining parts of Bihar i.e., in U.P. are characterised by medium to below medium stature, Mesocephalic head, mesorrhine nose and

Table- Somatometric Characters

Community	Place	Ethnic Status	Dialect/ Language- Family**	Sex	Number	ST.		Cl.		N.I.		T.F.I.		Reference
						X	S.E.	X	S.E.	X	S.E.	X	S.E.	
Bihar														
Brahman-Bhumihar	South Bihar	OC	Magahi-IA	M	121	167.14	5.83	75.87	3.71	-	-	89.46	5.00	Mitra, 1970
Brahman-Bhumihar	South Bihar	OC	Magahi-IA	-	58	167.27	7.40	77.00	0.50	69.00	0.80	86.80	0.60	Mitra, 1970
Brahman-Bhumihar	Patna	OC	Magahi-IA	M	85	164.4	-	76.60	-	69.00	-	-	-	Chakladar, 1936
Brahman-Bhuminhar	Bihar	OC	Hindi-IA	M	25	171.38	-	75.20	-	82.00	-	-	-	Chanda, 1916
Brahman-Bhuminhar	Nalanda	OC	Hindi-IA	M	58	167.20	3.78	77.01	0.51	69.04	0.76	86.77	0.56	Mitra, 1951 (unp.)
Brahman-Bhuminhar	Bihar	OC	Magahi-IA	M	121	167.14	5.30	75.87	0.34	67.40	0.60	89.46	0.45	Mitra, 1951 (unp.)

mesoprosopic face. The blood group picture in this region shows a decline in the frequency of gene B, with a corresponding increase in the frequency of O. Some other features which distinguish these populations from those of the North-west region are a relatively high incidence of O, R (CDC haplo type), ESD and PGM and low/r (cde haple type), Hp and PGD Gene.

The Aryan type in which Babhans are one of them, marked by a relatively long (dolichocephalic) head; a straight finely cut (lepto-rhine) nose, a long symmetrically narrow face, a well-developed forehead, regular features and a high facial angle. The stature is fairly high, ranging from 171.6 cm in Punjab to 165.6 cm in the Bengal province (including Bihar, Babhans) and the general build of the figure is well proportioned and slender rather than massive. Complexion of the caste is described as 'wheat coloured'.

Table given on page 48 present data on somatometric characters, viz. : Stat Index (C.I.), Nasal Index (N.I.), and total facial Index (T.F.I.) of Bhumihar Brahman caste. It also presents mean and standard error (S.E.) based on All India Anthropometric Survey data of the said caste.

The following table is a reproduction of Mr. Risley's statement of average nasal index and cephalic index in case of Bihar.

Table

Name of Caste	**Average Nasal Index**	**Average cephalic Index**
Brahman	73.2	74.9
Babhan	**74.0**	**76.7**
Goala	76.7	76.2
Kurmi	78.5	75.7

Contd...

Kahar	79.7	76.1
Bind	82.2	74.0
Maghaiya Dom	82.2	76.2
Dusadh	82.4	—
Chamar	82.8	76.0
Musahar	88.5	75.2

References

- Ghazipur Memo I., 43.
- Oldham ibid 1., 66.
- Hindu Tribes 1., 41 sq.
- Swami Sahajanand Saraswati belongs to this stream of Brahman.
- Azamgarh Settlement Report, 27, Sq.
- These probably includes a few of the Dravidian Bhumihars who were not seperately tabulated.

3

Socio-Economic and Cultural Dimension

Social Status of the Caste : In its crude form social status refers to one's social position among different castes in the society. Thus it is a relative term and one has to look Bhumihar Brahman caste in this context.

Owing probably to the controversy about origin, the social standing of the Babhans is not altogether easy to determine precisely, and varies slightly in different parts of the area which they inhabit. In south-eastern Bihar they rank immediately below Kayastha, but in Shahabad, Saran and the North-Western Provinces they appear to stand on much the same level as Rajputs. The facts that in Patna and Gaya the Amashtha or Karan Kayastha will eat kachcha food which has been cooked by a Babhan, while the other sub-caste of Kayasthas will not, may perhaps be a survival from times when Babhans occupied a higher position than they do at the present day. In Champaran, according to Mr Beames, Babhans are not permitted to drink and smoke with Brahmans, "and only under some restrictions with "Rajputs. Thus, a Rajput may eat rice with them only when it is "without condiments; he may not eat bread and he may drink water" only from an earthen vessel, not from a brass lota. Similarly, when "he eats with them his food must be placed on a dish made of leaves and not on the usual brass thali." The meaning of these "apparently trifling distinctions is that the Rajputs, on an emergency may eat hastily prepared food with them, but nothing that implies "a long preparation or deliberate intentions", Babhans themselves claim to observe a higher standard of ceremonial purity than Rajputs, in that they will not touch the handle (Parihath or Lagna) of the plough, and that they use the full Upanayan ritual when investing their children with the Janaue or sacred thread. In the matter of food they profess to take cooked food only with Brahmans and sweetmeats, curds, parched rice, etc (Pakki), from Rajputs and the group of castes from whose hands a Brahman can take water. As regards the latter class, they are careful to explain that, although they will take sweetmeats as guests in their houses, they will not sit down in their houses and eat with them. The Babhan's own diet is the same as that of all orthodox Hindus, and, like theirs, depends in some respects on consideration of sect. Thus Saivas and Saktas eat flesh while Vaishnavas are restricted to vegetarian food. Spirituous liquors are strictly forbidden and can only be indulged in secretly.

As the state got more and more pulled into the vortex of the market forces, changes did, inevitably, take place in social relations; but these changes have till today remained incomplete. Traditional systems have been breaking down, but modern systems have not yet been securely founded. Dining and intermingling of Babhans with other castes in the villages have increased but the mindset has not changed to that extent which is needed for speedy development and this has caused, in many, cases, agrarian tensions and discontent and the rise of private army (Brahmarshi Sena) within this caste.

Occupation

Determination of occupation of a caste depends on the geographical location and other factors attached to it. From time immemorial, the soil of the Gangetic valley is the most fertile one and from ancient period, castes settled around it took to agriculture as its main occupation. This confirm to the Nesfield's theory of caste, according to which, "Function and only function alone is the foundation upon which the whole caste system of India was built up." Till date Bihar and U.P., are essentially an agrarian state. In Bihar about 79.0 percent of the working population is directly dependant on agriculture, which contributes 59.0 percent to the gross domestic product originating from the state. The number of irrigation pump-sets and tubewells energized upto March, 1981 in at least five districts, where the caste Babhan/Bhumihar Brahmans resides, i.e., Gaya, Nalanda, Rohtas, Patna, Nawada and Munger, compared well with similar figures in the agriculturally most advanced districts in Punjab, Haryana, and Western Uttar Pradesh.

The characteristic occupation of the Babhan caste, as indeed is indicated by the title Bhumihar, is that of settled agriculturists; but they will under no circumstances drive the plough with their own hands. Apart from this special prohibition, they donot appear to be unreasonably fastidious as to how they get their living and will take service as soldiers, constables, durwans, Nagdis or Lathials, cut wood, work as coolies and do anything that is not specifically unclean. Many of them trade in grain, but it is considered derogatory to deal in miscellaneous articles or to go in for general shop-keeping. The Bhumihar emerged as Zamindars in the pre-colonial and colonial times. Some Babhans hold great estates in Bihar and the North-Western Provinces, among whom may be mentioned the Maharajas of Benaras, of Bettiah in Champaran, Tekari in Gaya, Hathwa in Saran and Tamakhi in Gorakhpur, the Raja of Sheohar, and the Rajkumar Babu of Madhoban in Champaran. They are found as tenure-holders of all grades, occupancy and non-occupancy raiyats, while a very few have sunk to the position of landless day-labourers. According to their own account, although ranking as Ashraf or high caste cultivators, they enjoy no special privileges in respect of rent, and are not particularly sought after as tenants, because, in common with Brahmans, Rajputs and Kayasths, they cannot be called upon for forced labour (begari) or for specific services in addition to the money-rent. The fact seems to be that, as they wili not plough themselves, and therefore, must employ labourers (Kamiyas) for this purpose, they cannot pay so high a rent as men who work with their own hands; while their bold and overbearing character, and their tendency to mass themselves in "strong and pugnacious brotherhoods" render them comparatively undesirable tenants in the eyes of an exacting landlord. It is said, indeed that the title Bhumihar, a term which Babhans never apply to themselves, has passed into a by word for sharpness and cunningness. In many cases the abolition of Zamindari had indiractly helped Bhumihar because the land went in their hand. Present day occupations are trading, business, government or private services etc., They also avail themselves of different rural employment programmes and other beneficial schemes. Overall the Babhans/Bhumihar emerged as a dominant community who remained primarily a community of middle-level peasants.

The ANS Institute at Patna with support from the ILO, initiated a detailed study of the dynamics of employment and poverty in Bihar in 1981. The survey was conducted from 1981 to 1983 and data pertaining to land ownership, input and output of crops, irrigation facilities, land improvement etc., in relation to caste, class and land in Bihar reveals that to a considerable extent medium to large land-holdings are still owned by some upper castes in Bihar, but the modern inputs into agriculture are not properly appropriated by them, hence low productivity. But this is not true about the middle castes as they have even production with smaller landholdings and lesser. Thus social background of the people engaged in agriculture becomes one of the most significant factors in agricultural production. These tables are given 56 to 54.

All these tables indicate that the peasant castes who themselves are working in the field are in better position than those landholding castes, who donot-work themselves in field. Most of the Bhumihar landholders donot work in the field, either they hire labours, or are share croppers in Bihar and this has direct bearing on crop productivity which in turn affects other things.

Property is distributed equally among the sons, while succession rights devolve upon the eldest one.

Jajmani system is still prevailing in most of the Bhumihar villages, where other castes get in cash or in kind reward for serving Bhumihars from time to time or when the need arises so.

The upper castes form only 13.22* per cent (Brahman: 4.7%, Rajput: 4.2%, Bhumihar: 2.9%

* Report of the Backward Classes Commission, Part-1 GOI, 1980.

Table

Land ownership by Caste Absolute Numbers and (in Brackets) Percentage Distribution of Households

Land Ownership Group (acres)	*Caste*									
	Brahmin+ Kayasta	*Bhumihar+ Rajput*	*Backward*	*Yadav*	*Koiri*	*Kurmi*	*Other Backward II*	*Scheduled Caste*	*Moslem*	*Total*
0	24	8	251	31	15	8	87	477	487	4087
	(2.2)	(0.7)	(23.1)	(2..9)	(1.4)	(0.7)	(8.0)	(43.8)	(17.2)	(43.1)
0-1	38	59	126	70	79	12	61	181	57	682
	(5.6)	(8.7)	(18.4)	(10.3)	(11.5)	(1.7)	(8.9)	(26.6)	(8.3)	(27.)
1.2.5	52	68	26	20	30	11	22	22	36	291
(18.0)	(23.4)	(8.9)	(6.9)	(10.2)	(3.6)	(7.4)	(7.4)	(11.5)	(11.5)	
2.5-5.0	80	51	3	18	11	20	7	6	20	217
(36.8)	(23.7)	(1.6)	(8.1)	(5.1)	(9.4)	(3.4)	(2.9)	(9.1)	(8.6)	
5.0-10.0	77	23	0	3	4	16	7	1	14	145
	(52.8)	(15.8)	(0.0)	(2.1)	(2.8)	(10.7)	(5.1)	(0.9)	(9.8)	(5.8)
10.0-20.0	40	24	6	2	1	4	2	0	4	82
	(48.5)	(29.3)	(6.9)	(2.1)	(1.4)	(4.6)	(2.1)	(0.0)	(5.1)	(3.2)
20+	8	8	0	0	0	1	2	0	1	20
	(41.5)	(41.2)	(0.0)	(0.0)	(0.0)	(4.1)	(8.8)	(0.0)	(4.4)	(0.8)
Total	318	241	412	144	140	70	188	692	319	2524
	(12.6)	(9.6)	(16.3)	(5.7)	(5.5)	(2.8)	(7.5)	(27.4)	(12.6)	(100.0)

No. of missing observations = 7

Above table reveals that in Bihar, besides SCs, OBCs, Bhumihar+Rajput occupies 9.6% of total land, but the land improvement is not so good among them as is shown in the table given below.

Table
Land Improvements in Different Types of Households (Bihar)

	% Area Improved with Irrigation (All sources)	Percentage Area Improved by Canal	Percentage Area Improvement by Govt. Tubewell	Percentage Area Improved by Pvt. Tubewell	Percentage Area Improved by other Irrigation Sources	Land Leveling (Acres)	Other Improvements (acres)
1	2	3	4	5	6	7	8
Size Class of Cultivated Land							
Upto 0.5 acre	0.0	0.0	0.0	0.0	0.0	0.005	0.0
0.5 to 1 acre	0.0	0.0	0.0	0.0	0.0	0.009	0.0
1 to 2 acres	1.32	0.0	0.0	100.0	0.0	0.009	0.0
2 to 5 acres	2.14	0.0	0.0	85.13	14.86	0.096	0.0
5 to 10 acres	3.25	8.75	18.43	72.35	0.0	0.050	0.0
10 and Above	0.57	0.0	0.0	0.0	100.0	0.060	1.56
Class							
Agricultural labour not tied	0.90	0.0	0.0	100.0	0.0	0.004	0.0
Agricultural labour tied	0.0	0.0	0.0	0.0	0.0	0.002	0.0
Poor Middle peasant	0.0	0.0	0.0	0.0	0.0	0.033	0.0
Middle Peasant	1.40	0.0	100.0	0.0	0.0	0.002	0.0
Big peasant	3.90	0.0	0.0	85.81	14.19	0.086	0.05
Land Lord	0.30	100.0	0.0	0.0	0.0	0.009	0.0
Non-agriculture	0.0	0.0	0.0	0.0	0.0	0.0	0.0

Contd...

Caste							
Brahmin and Kayasta	0.20	100.0	0.0	0.0	0.0	0.117	0.0
Bhumihar & Rajput	3.50	0.0	0.0	85.71	13.64	0.20	0.96
Backward I	0.0	0.0	0.0	0.0	100.0	0.005	0.0
Yadav	1.00	0.0	0.0	0.0	0.0	0.031	0.0
Koiri	0.0	0.0	0.0	0.0	0.0	0.046	0.0
Kurmi	11.40	0.0	20.24	79.76	0.0	0.0	0.0
Other Backward	0.0	0.0	0.0	0.0	0.0	0.017	0.0
Scheduled Caste	1.20	0.0	0.0	100.00	0.0	0.0	0.0
Muslim	0.0	0.0	0.0	0.0	0.0	0.001	0.0

* Big Peasants & Landlord includes Bhumihar in the state, but not always, many of them comes under middle peasant. These are used in relative terms.

Table
Different Types of Accumulation Among Different Types of Households (Bihar)

	Per acre value of modern capital goods	Total value of Machinary (per acre)	Per capita value of Grain stores	Per capita value of Cattle sheds	Per acre total value of Drought cattle	Per capita value of Bicycles	Per capita value of Radio
1	2	3	4	5	6	7	8
Size Class of Cultivated Land							
Upto 0.5 acre	0.0	236.833	3.285	0.142	1340.756	2332	0329
0.5 to 1 acre	49.563	213.716	4.738	8.200	799.144	7.830	1.099
1 to 2 acre	38.122	469.632	6383	51.010	606316	11.963	3.219
2 to 5 acres	136.607	402.138	6.878	62.066	287.267	9.144	6.786
5 to 10 acres	187324	533332	31.733	159.906	273.313	16.229	12.214
10 & above	294.464	488.482	27.837	121.262	209.436	17.394	
Class							
Agricultural labour not tied	34.789	171.514	1.433	11375	771.144	2.589	1.381
Agricultural labour tied	29.729	157.831	2.648	14334	1183.334	0.0	0.0
Poor Middle Peasant	90.143	629.283	8.419	31.594	645.754	6.670	4.857
Middle Peasant	160.528	512.211	5.422	50.141	343.555	11.455	6.060
Big Peasant	210.477	586.602	19377	91.147	347.994	15.230	7.462

Contd...

Land Lord	290.625	549.162	12.577	109.153	375.660	20.182	16.124
Non Agriculture	04	577.167	1.174	0360	0.0	7.299	0.0
Caste							
Brahmin & Kayasta	139.711	466.148	13.202	81496	362.349	17.710	9.575
Bhumihar & Rajput	296.667	562.730	14.869	46.703	372.703	14.261	6.713
Backward I	20.874	162.572	1.930	13.721	854.100	3.040	0.604
Yadav	0.0	184.496	5.822	97.410	243.384	10.833	6.561
Koiri	341.958	971.420	9.686	75.939	690.100	13.558	1.768
Kurmi	621.497	1662.243	74.175	278.906	438.997	15.514	16.378
Other Backward	15.107	182.009	2.472	37.598	474305	7.298	6.132
Scheduled Caste	112.971	212.877	2.206	5.598	1124.191	2.465	1.505

Bycycle and Radios as an indicators of the Process of modernisation of agrarian technology in various aspects have been included in the survey. Per capita ownership of these two items are on increase with the rise in Land improvement. In case of these two items, Bhumihar + Rajput hold third position.

Table

Extent and Source of Irrigation and Cropping Intensity Among Different Types of Households (Bihar)

	% of area irrigated to net sown area	Intensity of cropping	% of total area irrigated by canal	% of total area irrigated by tubewell	% of total area irrigated by other means
	1	2	3	4	5
Size of Cultivated Land					
Up to 0.5 acres	40.12	1.93	52.30	37.69	10.00
055 to 1 acres	33.35	1.61	33.82	44.85	2132
1 to 2 acres	43.76	1.62	42.64	47.64	9.71
2 to 5 acres	26.28	1.60	68.29	26.29	5.41
5 to 10 acres	44.93	1.69	52.97	41.32	5.71
10 to more acres	40.71	1.55	78.79	16.58	4.64
Class					
Agricultural labour not tied	52.45	1.49	83.80	12.15	4.05
Agricultural labour tied	59.01	1.58	61.51	38.49	0.0
Poor Middle peasant	32.61	1.84	2S.67	56.86	14.46
Middle peasant	35.29	1.60	71.58	20.72	7.70
Big peasant	41.04	1.74	52.58	39.73	7.69

Contd...

Land lord	38.57	1.75	69.16	26.93	3.92
Non Agriculture	0.0	0.0	0.0	0.0	0.0
Caste					
Brahmin +Kayasta	47.78	1.97	72.45	20.95	6.59
Bhumihar + Rajput	33.79	1.57	59.17	34.60	6.23
Backward I	37.08	1.58	84.94	13.08	1.98
Yadav	20.17	1.46	53.07	36.15	10.78
Koiri	7032	1.60	55.05	28.55	16,40
Kurmi	63.48	1.92	2.39	91.54	6.07
Other Backward II	68.72	1.59	80.16	12.91	6.93
Scheduled Caste	58.54	1.67	70.54	29.20	0.25
Muslim	56.68	1.56	32.96	67.04	0.0

Percentage of net sown area and intensity of cropping is least among Bhumihar + Rajput. Similarly, use of canal and tubewell for irrigation purpose is highest among BCs and Kurmi respectively. Here also Bhumihar + Rajput is lagging behind (canal - 59.17%, tubewell-34.60%)

Table

Details about Aggregated Input and Output (All crops) in Different Types of Households (Bihar)

	Total value Gross output (per acre)	Total cost of purchased seed (per acre)	Total cost of Purchased fertilizer (per acre)	Total cost of purchased (other) (per acre)	Total input cost (per acre)	Total value of marketed (per acre)
1	2	3	4	5	6	7
Size Class of Cultivated Land						
Upto 0.5 acre	2227.963	118.966	177.426	65.778	290.861	101.960
0.5 to 1 acre	2195.357	72.S33	98.320	57.711	288.944	34.210
1 to 2 acres	1766.230	51.118	135.207	63.981	244.657	70.856
2 to 5 acres	1569.033	32.749	120.650	30.677	178.123	120.472
5 to 10 acres	1571.680	—	123.111	43397	191.127	264.125
10 and more	1444.051	117.110	93.070	29.604	139.792	254.582
Class						
Agricultural labour not tied	1389.932	36.312	103.801	29.839	169.894	98.227
Agricultural labour tied	1978.150	42.549	122.298	44.570	207.594	60.905
Poor middle peasant	2177.361	101.325	177.620	66.275	314.448	66.070
Middle peasant	1731.939	20.442	150.354	44.987	215.970	48.603
Big peasant	1879.264	31.617	130355	26315	204.512	241.443
Land Lord	1264.796	27392	73.211	48.207	147.606	223.539

Contd...

Caste						
Brahmin + Kayasta	1624367	27.949	108.131	49.204	183-625	257.726
Bhumihar + Rajput	1817.490	44.222	117.678	37.297	198.209	201.413
Backward I	1693.085	37.680	113370	43.243	193.187	82.090
Yadav	1129.233	14.190	87.174	49.180	120.611	25.445
Koiri	2147.644	72.085	235.858	77.051	354.898	32.241
Kurmi	2727.615	23.904	299346	108.181	413-811	571056
Other Backward	1493.264	11.244	76328	44.394	131.985	59.893
Scheduled Caste	1882.070	53.847	121.172	32.320	205.702	120.856
Muslim	1214.280	25.108	86.735	30372	117.157	135.526

Detail of aggregate input and output of all crops show that Kurmi hold the position in total value marketed, whereas with 201.413 (per acre), Bhumihar + Rajput hold third position.

All the above tables indicate that those peasant castes who themselves are working in the field are in better position than those landholding castes who donot work themselves in the field. Most of the Bhumihars donot work in the field, either they hire labour or are share croppers in the State and this directly affects the crop productivity which in turn affects other things.

Table : Caste and Agricultural Occupations, Bihar, 1951*

	Brahmin	Rajput	Vaishya	Backward Classes	Scheduled Castes and Tribes	Tribals and Aboriginals	Others
No. of families	491	429	372	3,639	2,210	207	2,195
% of total No. of families	5.1	4.5	3.9	38.1	23.2	2.2	23.0
Land-owners	81 (71.84)	8.2 (6.32)	1.1 (0.72)	1.1 (7.22)	3.5 (13.90)	—	—
Tenants	—	78.6 (14.07)	31.7 (4.92)	44.0 (66.82)	15.4 (14.19)	—	—
Agricultural workers	—	6.3 (0.95)	18.0 (2.35)	35.2 (44.99)	66.6 (51.71)	—	—
Non-Agricultural workers	19.0 (6.96)	6.9 (2.25)	49.2 (13.68)	19.5 (53.10)	14.5 (24.01)	—	—
Total	100.0	100.0	100.0	99.8	100.0		

* Source : All India Agricultural Labour Enquiry, *Rural Manpower and Occupational Structure*, pp. 55-57. (The figures in parenthesis indicate the dispersion of each occupational category over various castes.)

Kayastha: 1.4%)) of the population of Bihar, but their dominance in Bihar life is much greater than their number would suggest. The numerical weakness of the upper castes is more than compensated by their ritual status, social prestige and economic power. In ritual matters the Brahmins enjoy the first position followed by the Bhumihar Brahmins and the Rajputs. The Kayasthas, although low on scale of the ritual status, have 'rivalled the above castes.

The picture has changed little if we accept the findings of the All-India Agricultural Labour Enquiry, which in 1951 conducted sample surveys over the entire country to discover the caste basis of agricultural occupations. The following table (on page 65) summarises its findings:

It is evident from the table that 78.16 per cent of land-owners are concentrated in two upper castes. The lower down in the caste hierarchy, the greater the extent to which lower castes depend for their living on farm labour. Only one upper caste, the Rajputs, constitute 0.95 per cent of the total agricultural labour force, as compared to the backward classes (44.99 per cent) and the scheduled castes and tribes (51.71 per cent). In other words, the economic position of a particular caste is highly correlated with its ritual status in the caste hierarchy. Moreover, the backward classes and scheduled castes do not own land to any significant extent, which increases their dependence for means of livelihood on the land-owning Brahmins and Rajputs.

Marriage and Customs

Before coming to marriage and custom related to Babhan, certain terms which have been used frequently should be dealt upon to clear the concept.

Mr. J.F. Mclennan introduced the term exogamy and endogamy in his essay on 'primitive marriage', for the first time. Exogamy is prohibition of marriage between all persons recognised as bring of the same blood, because of their common blood, - whether they form one community or part only of a community, or parts of several communities and accordingly it may prevent marriage between persons who are of different local castes, while it frequently happens that it leaves persons of the same local castes (who are not of the same blood) free to marry one another. Endogamy allows marriage only between persons who are recognised as being of the same blood connection or kindered, and if, where it occurs, it confines marriage to the caste or community, it is because the caste regard itself as comprising a kindered." Sir H. Maine in his book "Early Law and Customs" (p. 223) prescribed the marriage usages of the tribes and castes concerned in details.

Exogamous septs or sections are further classified into three distinct classes — (1) Totemistic, (2) Eponymous and, (3) Territorial.

(1) **Totemistic** : Confined for the most part to tribes and castes of Dravidian descent.

(2) **Eponymous** : It being either a vedic saint (as with Brahmans and the castes who imitate them) or a chief of comparatively modern date.

(3) **Territorial** : It refers either to some very early settlement of a section or to the birthplace of its founder, as is found in Babhans caste also.

Similarly endogamy work on the following ground:

(a) Ethnic groups, (b) Linguistic or provincial groups, (c) Territorial or Local groups, (d) Functional or Occupational groups, (e) Sectarian groups and (f) Social groups.

Marriage: Exogamy

Like the Rajputs, the Babhans exclude the section of both father and mother, or, in other words, forbid a man to marry a woman who belongs to the same section as he himself or his mother. The operation of this rule is further extended by the manner in which it is applied. Account is taken, not merely of the section to which the proposed bride herself belongs (i.e., her father's section), but also of her mother's section, so that the marriage will be barred if the bride's mother belonged to the same section as the bridegroom's mother, though, of course neither bride not bridegroom can be members of that sections. In respect of prohibited degrees, they follow the rules current among the Kayasths.

Endogamy

Among the Babhans of Bihar, as among the Rajputs, no endogamous divisions exist, and they also intermarry on terms of equality with the Babhans of the North-Western Provinces. Some sections, however, are reckoned inferior to the rest notably the Hararia, Kodaria and Bhusbarat mentioned above, regarding whom there is a saying in Bihar —

> "Hararia, Kodaria, Bhusbarat mare,
> to Tirhut ka paap hare."

In the north of Manbhum the Rampai and Domkatar sections are in such low repute that members of the other sections will not give their daughter in marriage to Rampai or Domkatar men, although they have no objection to taking wives from those sections themselves. Consequently in that part of the country Rampai and Domkatar Babhans can only get wives from each other, though their women can obtain husbands from all sections except their own. If the restrictions were carried a step further, and Babhans belonging to other sections interdicted from taking Rampai and Domkatar women to wife, those sections would be wholly cut off from the jus connubii and would in fact, if not in name, have hardened into a sub-caste to be quite exceptional but the point deserves notice as it tend to throw light on the obscure problem of the formation of sub-castes.

All Babhan who can afford to do so marry their daughter as infants, the bride's age being often no more than four or five years during British period. The same rule holds good for boys. Only they are married comparatively later in life, and a son unmarried at the age of puberty does not bring the same sort of reproach on the family as a daughter is supposed to do so. Instances, however, are not wanting where for special reasons the daughters of wealthy families have been married after they were groom up, as was the case with the late Maharani of Tekari, and it seems to be clear that even the most orthodox members of the caste do not take the extreme sacerdotal view of the necessity of infant-marriage.

Regarding infant marriage a scientific explanation has been given by Mr. John Nesfield in his article on the Tharus and Bogshar of Upper India. He says: In the oldest type of society a woman was exposed to a double evils — the stain of communism within her own clan so long as she remained there, and the risk of forcible abduction into an alien clan, where she became the wife-slave of the man who captured her. In Hindu custom, a girl was bethrothed at six or eight and married at ten or eleven. The betrothal ceremony is considered by all classes of the Hindu community to be of immense importance, and it made marriage binding, if not a father is publicly disgraced. [Betrothal : means "Mangni" that is, begging for a boy for until the boy had been secured, the girl was not safe"]. Another reasons may be due to insecurity of getting good boys.* Again it came into being due to under presure of social necessity; by the families of the highest group, who had the largest surplus of marriageable daughters. Caste complications demand that the ceremonial portion of the transfer shall be effected while she is still a child.

Ordinarily a price is paid for a bridegroom, but the purchase of brides is by no means uncommon. A man may marry two sisters and the number of wives he may have is subject to no limit except his ability to maintain them. Some say, however, that a second wife is only permissible if the first proves barren, is convicted of unchastity, or suffers from an incurable disease. Whatever may be the rule on the subject, it is rare to find a man with more than two wives. But now the monogamy system is followed, as civil marriage rule donot permit Biogamy. Widows are not allowed to marry again. Divorce is unknown : a faithless wife is simply turned out of the caste and left to shift for herself by becoming a Prostitute, turning mohammdan, or joining some of the less reputable religious sects.

Marriage Ceremony

The marriage ceremony of the Babhan doesnot appear to differ materially from the standard type of a Bihar marriage, which has been described by Mr. Griesson at page 362 of "Behar Peasant Life". The process of marriage starts with negotiation of bride's father with future groom's parents and when the marriage is settled thereafter, "Tilak" ceremony takes place and thus other cere-monies followed. It should perhaps be noted that a Babhans "Marhwa" or marriage shed has six post, not four, and that the bride is held throughout the ceremony by a woman of the Kahar caste. During erection of "Marhwa", nears and dears one of the girl parents participate and the ceremony of applying "Haldi" (oil mixed with turmeric) on the body of these peoples take place. The songs meant for this occasion is sung by the ladies. The end of this ceremony take place by distributing sweet or "prasad" to these peoples. During marriage ceremony every day has its own special occasion and songs for these occasion are sung by the village ladies including relatives. In the bride's house, a ceremony of digging earth soil (matkorah) take place. In this, the bride who wears an old sari is accompanied by a huge gathering of ladies who took her to nearby field for this purpose. In the way to the field, the songs are sung by these women accompanied by beating of drums, which is performed by a lower caste woman (chamar) of the village. Before marriage bride's body is applied with the paste of "haldi", Similarly in the bridegroom's home in Babhans, "Patkati" or "Barkati" (cutting of tree branches/leaves with the help of sword) takes place. He is accompanied by the village women/relatives to the tree. A day before the wedding day the brethren are entertained at a feast (Bhatwan). They are also fed on the morning when the procession starts. Next comes the "Imlighotna which is done by bride's mother's brother. On the day of marriage groom's wear "Mour" a headgear made of mettalic wires and threads of delicate designs, which is gaudy and colourful. Partilocal residence is in vogue in Babhan. In some cases the thread ceremony takes place (at the age of eight to ten years) in which the groom's/boy who is being initiated begs from a woman whom he addresses "mother". He is leaving for Kashi to begin his studies. This what the lady asks of the boy who begs :

> O, my child, what would you have 'Dhoti' or
> book, or the saffron thread do you desire ?

O, my child, would you have gold as gift or
the thread (you wear) on your shoulders ?

During this ceremony the boy carries a stick of palasa-wood, and wears a loin-cloth of 'Munja' grass and a deer-skin. This austere dress of the Brahmachari is described in one or two teh songs. Says a woman:

O, go forth in the forest, e'en the blades of grass are still and the tiger roars not,

O, out with a stick of 'Palasa' and seek a deer-skin.

The marriage procession of the bridegroom's arrives with pomp and splendour at the house of the bride's father, while the women sing :

whence comes the decorated tusker,
whence such fine robes ?

whence comes the prince to marry,
diadem on his forehead, betel in mouth ?

From Gorakhpur comes the tusker,
the fine robes from Patna.

The prince of Kashi has come to marry,
diadem on his forehead, betel in mouth.

According to Hindu Law the completion of the seventh step by the bride renders the marriage final and irrevocable, a number of Babhans in Patna division in their opinion, "Sindurdan", or the smearing of vermilion on the parting of the bride's hair, formed the binding portion of the ceremony — not the circumambulation of the sacrificial fire (Bhanwar or Bedi Ghumaeh), which in Bihar (including Jharkhand) takes the place of the Vedic Saptapadi. If the bridegroom were to die after "Bhanwar" and before "Sindurdan", the bride would not be deemed a widow, and would be permitted to marry another man. The custom of "Sindurdan" as probably been borrowed from the marriage service of the non-Aryan races. After marriage, the bride's accompanying with groom's arrives at the house of bridegroom's, where some ceremony takes place and "Kohbar" is one of them. At bride-groom house ceremony of eating boiled rice and pulse take place, along with vegetables and sweet-curd.

Briefly we can say that the community has lineages, gotras and sub-groups. Their gotras, muls and subgroups regulate marriage alliances, while lineages indicate ancestry. The two main gotras reported among them are Bhardwaj and Shandilya. They use Mishra, Pandey, Sharma, and Sahi as surnames. The marriage rule is endogamy at the community level and exogamy at the village, gotra, mul and lineage levels. The child marriage followed by gaona has been replaced by adult marriage now-a-days and the mode of acquiring spouses is through negotiation. Monogamy is the form of marriage. A bindi, vermilon and bangles are the symbols of married women. Remarriage of a widower is permissible and in few cases widow marriages also take place but this is a rare phenomenon. Both junior levirate and junior Sororate are permitted. Dowry is given in cash and kind, and the rule of residence after marriage is partrilocal. Men of this caste wore bala or bali in Shahabad and 'Kanausi' in Patna and Gaya districts, which has now-a-days came under fashion in every castes.

In nutshell, some of their important marriage rituals are, Chekai, Faldan, Tilak, Dwarpuja, Dhanbatti, Matkora Chumaun, Othangar, Sindurdan, Kohbar, etc.

During the 70's, the prosperous mauritian politician vied with one another to get their daughter married into respectful Bhumihar families of Bihar, who has prospered and one of the ways of their assertion of status was the amount of dowry they paid for their daughters. The situation got so out of hand for those Bhumihar who could not comete the dowry stakes began kidnapping grooms and getting them forcibly married off. The Babhans might marry two sisters and the numbers of wives depended upon their ability to maintain them previously, but not now.

Child Birth

Certain pre and post-delivery restrictions are observed by the Babhans. Normally the pollution period ends on the sixth day after delivery, but a nursing mother is confined in a room (saur) for twenty-one days. The twelfth day ritual (Barhi), the naming and first cereal feeding (Anna prashan) ceremonies are observed by Babhans. Child birth and specially the birth of a male child is celebrated with great pomp and splendour in the Babhans family. During this period "Sohar" and "Khelauna" takes place. The young woman experiencing the agonies of child birth, the mother-in-law soliciting the well-being of the daughter-in-law, the husband running to fetch the midwife, the midwife demanding princely gift, these are the principal themes of the "Sohar", while those of "Khelauna" are the cries of the newborn baby, the ecstasy of the mother, the happiness of the mother-in-law and the joy of the father, who is ready to distribute all that they possesses in gifts. When a son is born at long last after much prayer, the mother-in-law describes her happiness thus :

What joy the son is born,
I sing the auspicious song.
Long may the child live,
I shall see him and be happy.
My son's wife is mother now,

Joys knows no bounds.
I shall carry the child in my arms,
laugh and play with it.

Here is a song which describes the younger sister of the husband to her sister-in-law on the occasions of Sohar (on the birth of a son) :-

"I shan't accept this simple sari,
I must have a colourful petticoat,
O my brother's wife.
Nor this blouse,
I must have a chemise of dappled cloth,
O my brother's wife!
No, I shan't accept either bracelets or armlets:
I shall only accept a pair of scintillating ear-rings,
O my brother's wife!"

"Chhati" or the auspicious "sixth day" is observed by Babhans and nears and dears ones are invited on this very occasion to celebrate it.

A Brahman Priest (Pandit) is invited to perform the naming ceremony. The Tonsure (Mundan) ceremony is observed for both male and female children. The ears of girls are pierced (Karna chhedan) at the age of three or four years.

Disposal of the dead

Babhans burn their dead and perform the Sraddh Ceremony on the eleventh day after death in the fashion described by Mr. Grierson ("Behar Peasant life," page 391) Some are mentioned here : first of all Ganga Jal is poured in death mouth. After that dead body is prepared for taking it to burial ground. Almost in all cases, Babhans are buried on a river bank. All those who participate in it got tonsure (mundane) their head. After returning from the river bank, they take some foods. After that the main person who has performed Sraddh Ceremony, wears the white dhoti till the end of this ceremony. In between some other ceremonies take place. In cases of extreme poverty the corpse is thrown into a river after the nearest relative has touched the mouth with a burning torch. At the Sraddh ceremony, as in all other acts of domestic worship for which the services of a purohit are required. Kannaujia Brahmans officiate without thereby incurring any degradation in comparison with the Brahmans who serves the higher castes. In some parts of Eastern Bihar, Maithil Brahmans are employed by the Babhans. These rank below Kannaujias, and are looked down upon by the Srotriya Brahmans, not because they serve in Babhans houses, but because their own origin is believed to be of doubtful purity.

Babhan offer pinddan for peace of their deceased one's during "pitripaksha," the first fortnight of the Hindu month of Ashwin, corresponding to September-October on the bank of river Phalgu in Gaya. [Every year].

In nutshell, the dead are cremated and the Daswan, Terahwi, and Sraddh rituals are observed.

Religion

From the etymological point of view, Bouquet has shown, that religion is derived from the Latin word rel (L) igio; which itself is derived from either the root leg–, which means 'to gather', count or observe', or from the root lig– which means 'to bind'. In the former sense the implication is belief in, and observation of, signs of divine communication. In the latter sense the implication is the performance of necessary actions which may bind together man and the supernatural powers that be. Both the implications are relevant in view of the fact that beliefs and rituals have been found to be the main component parts of religions everywhere.

We all possess a vague notion of what is called religious which suffices for all practical purposes, but it should have some purposive meaning, that is why, Prof. Max Muller's treatise on the origin of religions try to define it. In his "Science of Religion", he gives the following definition :-

> "Religion is a mental faculty of disposition which, independent of, nay, in spite of sense and reason, enables man to apprehend the infinite under different names and under varying disguises."

In its other aspect, it can be defined only as the sum total of the beliefs, sentiments, and practices to which the laity are led by priestly influence and art.

In fact there is hardly a single religion in the world which is based on infallible knowledge or unexceptionable morality. Considering the forms of faith with which we are acquints it seems impossible to define religion in any other way than as mentioned above.

It is believed by most man that religions has its origin in the will of Divine Providences but a careful examination of the tenents of the several religions would lead inevitably to the conclusions that our faith have had their source in human Policy and not in divine will.

The religion of the Babhans, like that of the ordinary high-caste Hindu, conforms in its details to the ritual of whatever recognised sect he happens to belong to. Representatives of all sects are found amongst the caste in much the same proportion as in the population at large. Vaishnavism, however, is said to have been only recently introduced among them, and in North Bihar most Babhans are either Saivas or Saktas. No social consequences are involved by professing the tenents of any of the regular sects, and intermarriage between their members goes on freely within the limits of the caste. Besides the standard worship which a Babhan performs in virtue of belonging to a particular sect, all householders offer he-goats and rams to Kali on the 24th or 25th of Kaur (September-October), sweatmeats, sandal-paste, flowers to sitala on the 24th chait (March-April) and sugared cakes to Hanuman on every Tuesday. On the 1st of chait these three deities are propitiated with "Puwa (wheat-flour and molasses cooked in oil), 'Bara' (cakes of urid fried in oil), and 'Kachwania' (round balls of rice-flour, sugar, and butter). These offerings are presented by the men to the family without the aid of a Brahman, and are afterwards divided among the members of the households. Women are relegated to the task of appeasing a lower order of Gods-Hardiya, Bandi Mai, Sokha and Goraiya-with molasses and pitha, a sort of boiled pudding made of Sattu or Meal. The Babhan propitiate family and village dieties like Satisthan, chamundasthan and Harlakshmi. Sacred specialists from other communities conduct their life-cycle rituals. They observe festivals like Teej, Jiutia, Karva chauth, Bhai Dooj, and Godhan etc; The community has oral traditions in the form of folk-songs, folk-lore, and folk-tales.

Due to impact of urbanization, industrialization and modernization, many of the old rituals are not observed in toto and some have been modified to suit the requirements of present day.

At present, they are non-vegetarian and vegetarian both and mostly consume wheat and rice as their staple cereal diet. Now in Babhans, there is no organisation for the detection and punishment of breaches of caste rules. Action has to be taken by members on their own initiative. If the offence is open and well known, they at once cease to have any contact-with the offenders. If it is doubtful, an informal gathering of the influential people of the caste discusses the issue and chalks out a line of action. The burden of proof of innocence is on the suspected person. If found guilty, penalties are prescribed after consulting pandits and ceremonies of expiation have to be performed. Among the purificatory penances, mention may be made of, (i) going on pilgrimage for an appointed period, (ii) bathing in the Ganga and swallowing its sand, (iii) living on alms for a prescribed time, (iv) remaining silent for an appointed time, (v) taking only one meal in twenty-four hours, (vi) swallowing a mixture of five products of the cow (Panchgavya) and (vii) fasting. Ceremonies for expiation consists of sacrifice, worship of Satyanarayan, making gift of a cow, heifer and so on, to the family priest and feeding Brahmanas and fellow castemen.

Language and Literature

Magadhi languages in different regions have been grouped as Bihari languages by Dr. Grierson, the noted linguistic authority on Indian languages and are spoken by Babhans in the state. In this category he has included Magahi, Maithili and Bhojpuri. Magahi is the language of the Magadh tract of undivided Bihar, i.e. districts of Patna, Gaya, Jehanabad, Hazaribagh and Western parts of Palamu district. In some parts of Munger and Bhagalpur also Magadhi is used. Maithili is spoken in Darbhanga district. However with slightly varying forms it is also spoken in some parts of Purnea, Saharsha, Bhagalpur and Muzaffarpur districts. Similarly, Bhojpuri is spoken in East and West Champaran, Shahabad, Palamu, old Saran districts and also in the Eastern parts of Uttar Pradesh.

Moving descriptions of all the aspects of popular life are to be found in Magahi and Bhojpuri folk songs, There are a host of songs which describes the ecstasy of spring, the jhoola during rainy season, the pangs of seperation, the bickerings of daughters-in-law, the affection of brothers and sisters and parents for their children. Eminent literattures like Ram tavkya Sharma, Nalin Vilochan Sharma etc., have contributed a lot for development of hindi literature. In Bhojpuri, 'Birha', depicting the sentiments of menfolk and 'Batohia' written by Raghubir Narayan and the play entitled 'Bidesia' by Bhikhari Thakur have made history by their popularity. Bhikhari Thakur was the people's poet of Bhojpuri and in his poems are reflected the joys and sorrows, the toils and tears of the simple rural folk of his area. "Bibbo Ka Bibboka" written by Nalin vilochan Sharma early in the present decade, is the first full length poetic drama in Hindi on the lines of T.S. Eliot. Ram Krishna Benipuri wrote a number of popular plays to his credit. A few books on Magahi language has also been written. Nakchadi Tewari of Dumraon had written poetry in Brajabhsha. Legendary Magahi poet, Mathura Prasad Navin has written about the prevailing culture in the State, i.e.;

"Hamar gaon hai ala babua,
Hamar gaon hai ala,
Beta hai bandook uthawale,
Baap Jape hai mala"

(My world unique: the son carries a gun, the father counts his rosary). Nothing could express the bottom-line in Bihar better than this.

References

- Calcutta Review, January 1885
- Papers relating to infant Marriage and Enforced Widowhood in India, p. 178.

4

Caste and Politics

The word 'Politics', owes its origin to the Greek word 'Polis'. According to contemporary school, politics is 'termed as a struggle for power'. Different scholars have defined interaction between the caste and the politics in different ways. As Morris Jones observes that in recent years "Politics is more important to caste and caste is more important to politics". According to Leach, caste and politics are antithetical whereas M.N. Srinivas shows that caste has become an "Organised Vote-bank". As he writes "the power and activity of caste has increased in proportion as political power passed increasingly to the people from the rulers.

Politics is a competitive enterprise, its purpose is the acquisition of power for the realisation of certain goals, and its process is the one of identifying and manipulating existing and emerging allegiances in order to mobilise and consolidate positions. The important thing is organisation and caste structure provides one such organisational clusters along which the bulk of the population is found to live, politics must strive to organise through such a structure. Politics also finds material for its articulation in it. Caste and kin groups on the other hand, get a chance to assert their identity and to strive for positions. The Caste-politics problem in India is not a problem of definition but clearly one of empirical understanding of a competitive and mobile system which could give us a reasonable mode of caste and social dynamics.

From Karl Marx to Thorston Veblen, society struggle for subsistence has been described in various ways. Caste groups are already competing against one another in the political arena on the basis of growing inequality. This relative strength is determined increasingly not by their ritual status but by numbers, organisational strength and quality of leadership. The privileges enjoyed by the lowest-caste group in some areas are proofs of the new trends.

The crucial connecting link, however, between social stratification and the political system is political party, caste association or movement. A political party consists of "those whose entrepreneurial activities are essentially devoted to the recruitment of followers who attempt to modify the system either by participation in government or by directing their action against it.

The caste association, a voluntary organization composed of members from a single caste, was also viewed by political scientists as a potentially important political instrument. The caste association could demand candidacies or concessions in return for support by the caste. Also, through the association the urban politically-literate elite were linked with the less literate villagers belonging to the same caste.

Caste associations linking members of a caste within a region first emerged in the nineteenth century. Such associations became possible as education became more accessible and easier means of communication and transportation were established (trains, roads, printing presses, postal service etc.). Often, the associations were funded by western-educated male members. These organizations published newspapers and held conferences to discuss discrimination suffered, reform of customs, and the establishment of benefits such as scholarships and hostels (dormitories) for their student members.

Caste-fellows feel it their proud duty to strengthen the caste-organisation, remembering their obligations to it. Thus a vicious Circle has been created. The feeling of caste-solidarity is now so strong that it is truely described as caste-patriotism. Caste-consciousness has become more sharp due to enterance of political elements in it. Perhaps the earliest of such organisations is the one started by a Bihar Caste in 1891 (Memorendum for the Indian statutory commission, Bihar and Orissa, p. 87). Bhumihar Mahasabha has been active since 1896. And at present in the name of Swami Sahajanand Saraswati, such organisations are working in different parts of Bihar, Jharkhand and adjoining parts, i.e., in U.P. Now the Organisation has become more of political in nature than a social organisation. Some recent development have been observed, which are as follows:-

(a) The caste sentiment is being made deep-rooted by organising activities for children, women, farmers, working classes etc.;

(b) These associations have introduced the principle of election and elect office-bearers for day to day functioning.

(c) It has been made more definite by framing written constitutions and rules for caste-association.

(d) Efforts are being made by it to get facilities from the Government for benefit of caste in general

(e) The frequency of all caste members coming together has increased in recent years. Now all caste members assemble at one place or others for attending social, religious and national functions which further increases ties among them.

(f) Regular donation is collected from its members for different activities of the association.

R.S. Khare's study of the *Kanyakubja* Brahman association, for example, revealed that this organization had not engaged "either in any 'protective' or protest politics for mobility or for modernization".

A caste association must solve a number of problems if it is to be successful in politics. First, the population is fragmented into so many castes that even a dominant caste in a region does not constitute a majority of the electorate. Second, a few castes are organized adequately to mobilize all members of the caste to vote as a block. An association's ability to deliver the vote can be undermined rather easily by the opposition parties' putting up candidates from the same caste. Also, since it is narrowly identified with one caste, the organization cannot attract the support of voters of other castes unless it abolishes its exclusiveness and thus ceases to be a caste association.

Three Stages in the Relationship Between Caste and Politics

Rajni Kothari, a political scientist, has specified three typical stages in the relationship between caste and politics in a region.

Stage 1: This involves the politicization of a powerful elite caste, usually one which responded earliest to the opportunities for western education. In Maharashtra and Tamil Nadu, this was the Brahmans; in Bihar, it was the *Kaysthas* (traditionally scribes). With some political success on the part of the entrenched caste, the members of other high castes in the area would respond with resentment, feelings of relative deprivation, and possibly antagonism. These castes then challenge the entrenched caste as what Kothari calls an "ascendant caste". As in Bihar, it was Bhumihar Brahman who challenged the Kayasthas with the help of other castes. In three example given in Kothari's edited book, the ascendant caste is one of respectable cultivators who had been slower than the entrenched caste in accepting western education. In Rajasthan, the Rajputs were the entrenched, and the Jat cultivators the ascendant caste. In Tamil Nadu, the Brahmans were the entrenched, and the Shudra non-Brahmans were ascendant and in Maharashtra, the Brahmans were the entrenched, and the Marathas were the ascendant.

Stage 2 : Factionalism and fragmentation take place within the competing castes, and multi-caste and multi-factional alignments develop. Lower castes are often brought in to support high caste leaders and to strengthen a faction.

Stage 3 : Caste identity tends to languish with the progress in education, urbanization, and the development of an orientation toward individual achievement and modern status symbols. Individuals participate in networks which include persons of several castes. In Kothari's words, "The structure of particularistic loyalties" has been "overlaid by a more sophisticated system of social and political participation with crosscutting allegiances. Institutional differentiation and specialization has progressed, so that economic, political, educational institutions are distinctly different".

The Indian sociologist, G.S. Ghurye, raised the spectre of a future with Indian society fixed in Stage 2 — composed of a few blocks or coalitions of castes. This could occur through the gradual breakdown of rules of exogamy between castes of neighbouring rank, so that each connubium was enlarged to include several castes of adjoining rank. If this happened, the French social anthropologist, Louis Dumont, sees a result that:

> would be disastrous, for one would end up by aggregating a multitude of small groups into a few large blocks, which would be mutually hostile and exclusive to a dangerous degree.

Dumont believes that such blocks of castes would not be ranked or interdependent, but would be, rather:

> a universe of impenetrable blocks, self-sufficient, essentially identical and in competition with one another.

Whether Ghurye's or Kothari's vision is correct is hard to say. Kothari suggests that identifications other than that of caste are likely to become more important with advancing education, urbanization, and adoption of a modern achievement-orientation. Andre Beteille has pointed out, for example, that among the westernized elite, school-ties are much more important than caste ties. Salient identifications do not accumulate and crystallize in the modern sector as they did in the traditional. In the India of today, all of an individual's relationships are not channeled in caste grooves.

A process of fusion of castes resulting in only a few contending caste blocks could take place only if other bases of alignment between people, fan.ilies, and groups were consistently in abeyance – a rather unlikely condition. If all castes were distributed among a few major blocks contending for power through election and governmental institutions, there would be a new caste system based on a principle of competition.

(a) Bhumihar Caste and Politics

The relationship between caste and politics in context of Bihar and Bhumihar caste has been described below :-

The creation of Bihar and Orissa as separate provinces in 1912 was in a way a testimonial to the success of combining the caste and politics. Kayasthas got the opportunity of new openings of employment in various fields specially in politics in the state, this was not acceptable to other caste people, especially to Bhumihars. The leader of Bhumihars like Late Sh. S.K. Sinha began to organise his caste people to participate in politics in a big way; but Kayasthas want to maintain their supremacy in the politics, so they adopted the policy of divide and rule. In 1930, three caste groups were active - Kayasthas and Rajputs on the one hand and Bhumihars on the other.

It will be not out of the context to mention here that in 1937, the Bihar Legislative Assembly came into existence with a strength of 152 members. After independence, during first general election of 1952, 330 MLAs were elected on the basis of adult franchise and one member was nominated. The present strength which was raised in 1977 consists of 324 elected members of Legislative Assembly and 96 members for Legislative Council. After creation of Jharkhand, 80 seats went in their share.

By the time Congress formed its government in 1937, under the Act of 1935, the Bihar Congress had become polarised into two factions, one was headed by Sh. S.K. Sinha, a Bhumihar leader from Munger district and the other faction led by Sh. A.N. Sinha, a Rajput leader from South-Western Gaya district. Due to reluctance for fighting for Chief Minister Post, Sh. A.N. Sinha decided not to contest and the coveted post went to Sh. S.K. Sinha, who remained Bihar's Chief Minister till his death in 1961.

In 1957 election, when congress returned with majority, again Sh. S.K. Sinha became the Chief Minister due to majority of Bhumihars (besides Rajputs) in the Bihar Vidhan Sabha, as shown below in the Table :-

Table 1 : *Percentage of Caste composition of different Castes MLAs; on different assembly election

Castes groups	1957	1962	1967	1969	1972	1977
Brahmins	9.54	17.20	13.20	12.30	18.30	7.60
Bhumihars	16.19	12.60	14.80	14.60	14.70	14.80
Rajputs	14.20	23.60	22.20	28.50	19.80	21.70
Kayasthas	4.28	5.40	4.90	3.30	2.00	4.40
Total upper castes	44.25	59.00	53.00	53.90	54.80	48.60
Total other castes	55.75	41.00	47.00	46.10	45.20	51.40
Total	100.00	100.00	100.00	100.00	100.00	100.00

* Source : Economic and Political Weekly, February 14, 1977 and January 19, 1980.

After the death of both the factional leaders, the caste based politics of Bihar was headed by their respective juniors Sh. K.B. Sahaya and Sh. M.P. Sinha and they began to manoeuvre openly for Chief Minister post. In this contest Sh. Sahaya favoured Sh. B.N. Jha, who became the second Chief Minister of Bihar.

The table given below shows that the Council of Ministers was predominantly composed of upper caste members during the time of upper caste Chief Minister, Sh. M.P. Sinha. 13 out of 21 ministers belonged to upper castes whereas during backward caste Chief Minister Sh. B.P. Mandal, 9 out of 38 ministers belonged to upper caste

Table 2 : *Social composition of U.F. Minister at the time of Sh. M.P. Sinha and Sh. B.P. Mandal Chief Ministership.

Castes	No. of Minister during M.P. Sinha time	During B.P. Mandal time
Rajput	5	6
Brahmin	3	nil
Bhumihar	4	3
Kayastha	1	nil
others	8	29
	21	38

* Source : Economic and Political Weekly, February 14, 1977 and January 19, 1980.

Between 1934 and 1960 percentage of Kayasthas members in Bihar Pradesh Executive committee declined steeply from 53.84% to 4.76% and that of Bhumihar increased from 15.38% to 28.56%.

After this election the politics of Bihar became so caste-ridden that no political party got a clear majority with the result that in the beginning a new coalition ministry consisting of S.S.P., P.S.P., C.P.I., B.K.D., B.J.S. and Jharkhand begin to operate soon under the leadership of Sh. M.P. Sinha, a Bhumihar leader. Later on in 1968 Sh. B.P. Mandal became the first backward Chief Minister of the state, and at present the coaliation government is ruling the state with RJD having the upper hand (with Congress party). For example, in Siwan Parliamentary Constituency, (Sh.) Md. Shahbuddin* is contensting

Table 3 : *Caste Composition of the Bihar Pradesh Congress Executive Committee*, 1934-1962 (*in percent*)

Castes	1934	1935	1936	1937	1938	1939	1940	1942	1946
Upper Castes									
Brahmin	—	—	—	—	7.15	—	13/34	14.28	6.66
Bhumihar Brahmin	15.38	35.72	23.07	23.53	7.15	13.34	13.34	21.43	20.00
Rajput	7.70	14.28	23.08	17.63	21.42	26.67	26.67	28.58	26.68
Kayastha	53.84	28.57	29.41	23.53	35.70	26.67	6.66	7.15	20.00
Sub-total	76.92	78.57	75.56	64.69	64.27	66.68	60.01	71.44	73.34
Others									
Lower Castes	—	—	7.70	5.88	—	—	—	—	—
Scheduled Castes	—	—	—	—	—	—	6.66	7.15	—
Scheduled Tribes	—	—	—	—	—	6.66	—	—	—
Sub-total	—	—	7.70	5.88	—	6.66	6.66	7.15	—
Muslims	23.08	14.28	15.38	11.77	14.28	20.00	26.67	21.41	20.00
Not known and others	—	7.15	7.70	11.76	14.30	6.66	6.66	—	6.66
Total	100.00	100.00	100.00	100.00	100.00	100.00	100.00	100.00	100.00
Cases	13	14	13	17	14	15	15	14	15

Table 3 Contd. : *Caste Composition of the Bihar Pradesh Congress Executive Committee,* 1934-1962 *(in percent)*

Castes	1947	1948	1950	1952	1954	1955	1958	1960
Upper Castes								
Brahmin	7.15	9.52	12.50	21.05	10.53	15.00	14.28	14.29
Bhumihar Brahmin	14.28	14.29	12.50	21.05	21.05	20.00	23.81	28.56
Rajput	35.71	23.82	37.58	26.33	21.05	20.00	19.15	14.29
Kayastha	21.43	14.29	12.50	5.26	5.26	5.00	9.53	4.76
Sub-total	78.59	61.92	75.00	73.69	57.89	60.00	66.67	61.90
Others								
Lower Castes	—	19.04	12.50	10.53	21.05	20.00	14.28	14.29
Scheduled Castes	—	4.76	6.25	5.26	5.26	5.00	4.76	4.76
Scheduled Tribes	7.15	4.76	—	5.26	6.26	—	—	—
Sub-total	7.15	28.56	18.75	21.05	31.57	25.00	19.04	19.05
Muslims	14.28	9.52	6.25	5.26	5.26	5.00	9.53	14.29
Not known and others	—	—	—	—	5.26	10.00	4.76	4.76
Total	100.00	100.00	100.00	100.00	100.00	100.00	100.00	100.00
Cases	14	21	16	19	19	19	21	21

Table 4 : *Caste Composition of Population (Projected for 1961) and Active Congress Members in the Districts of Saharsa, Shahabad, Saran and Darbhanga*

Castes*	Saharsa			Shahabad		Saran		Darbhanga	
	Population 1956 N=585	Active Members 1961 N=78	Active Members 1961 N=191	Population 1961 N=152	Active Members 1961 N=244	Population	Active Members	Population	Active Members
Upper Castes									
Brahmin	4.80	23.42	15.38	10.00	22.51	7.11	12.50	10.15	27.86
Bhumihar Brahmin	1.00	1.20	2.56	3.07	7.33	3.84	14.47	1.55	6.56
Rajput	3.75	29.73	21.80	11.69	19.37	10.11	19.73	2.82	20.90
Kayastha	0.45	1.20	6.41	1.83	7.86	1.59	2.63	1.28	4.09
Total	10.00	55.55	46.15 26.59	57.07	22.65	49.33	15.80	59.41	
Lower Castes	66.08	29.06	23.07	49.87	17.27	55.02	21.71	56.33	14.24
Scheduled Castes	17.18	2.40	17.94	16.01	7.33	10.33	5.27	14.67	13.30
Muslims	6.30	3.99	2.56	6.90	2.62	12.00	6.59	13.20	8.19

* Other minor castes and cases not known have been left out

election 2004 but other castes including Bhumihars of the areas is supporting him. Similarly, the upper caste vote (Bhumihar : 1.25 Lakh), (Rajput : 80,000) is fragmented in Muzaffarpur Constituency. This has led to the defeat of Bhumihars four times (1977, 1980, 1989 and 1991) in the past at the hand of George Fernandes* which in turn end the political career of Niteshwar Prasad Singh (1977), Digvijay Narain Singh (1980), L.P. Shahi (1989) and Raghunath Pandey (1991). None of these Bhumihar leaders could bounce back.

Regarding Bihar Walter Hauser aptly observes : this meant that Bhumihars, Rajputs and Brahmins saw successive opportunities for their attractions to politics provided by the non-cooperation movement of 1920 and the civil disobedience movement of 1930 and 1932. As land holders of moderate means, these groups were financially capable of providing education to their son, and when the time came, of supporting a family member in political field.

In the year 1990, during the tenure of former Prime Minister Sh. V.P. Singh, Mandal Commission report giving 27.0 percent reservation to OBCs changed the shape of Indian polity from a two party systems to a multi dimensional structure in which every caste and sub-caste pushed and shoved for its own share of the political space. This led to the emergence of caste specific parties and now the caste groups are already competing against one another in the political arena on the basis of growing in - equality. Their relative strength is determined increasingly not by their ritual status but by numbers, organisational strength, quality and alliances and counter-alliances, the competing caste groups, by coopting men from politically inarticulate castes to position of second rank leadership, who in due course emerged as leaders in their own right, brought more and more castes into the vortex of politics.

* won election

The 1999 elections present a new facet of caste: under the umbrella of the B.J.P. regional caste groupings have attempted to create an all India polity and in Bihar the said caste alligned with regional political party for its share in national politics.

In the year, 2003, a rally of Brahmarshi Sangh had been organised at Patna Gandhi Maidan to celebrate Swami Sahajanand Saraswati, 114th Jayanti, by the Health Minister of Bihar Dr. Akhilesh Prasad Singh to draw political mileage out of it. Caste politics is such that Nikhil Chaudhary was ousted from ministership due to certain caste problems. Another important MLC of this caste is Dr. Mahachander Prasad Singh. Dr. C.P. Thakur hold the post of State Minister in the Central Government from Bihar in previous Lok Sabha but in the 14th Lok Sabha election he losts to Sh. R.K. Yadav of RJD. He had won previously the Parliament election from Bhumihar dominated Patna Lok Sabha. After lots of hue and cry by the caste fellow statue of Swami Sahajanand was installed at Harmu Road, Ranchi (Jharkhand).

During 80's, when anti-reservation stir took place, initially Bhumihars were the most-active which later culminated in castes war in Bihar due to Laloo Yadav's inertia in tackling the situation. What was most shocking in Bihar was the extent to which then Chief Minister Laloo Prasad Yadav encouraged the Yadavs to cross swords with the anti-reservation Bhumihars with the matters coming to a lead at the Pro-Reservation Sadbhavana Rally in Patna on October 8, 1990. At that time Ramvilas Paswan inflammatory speech at Bhumihar-Brahmin combine meeting resulted in a fresh round of violence which embol-dened Yadavs assaulting the then S.P., of Madhepura district. After SC Judgement of 16th November, 1991, the Congress Leaders like Mr. Ramjatan Sinha and Mr. Mahachandra Prasad Singh, who were active in the agitation, maintained low profile.

Kapildeo Singh, 80, a Bhumihar in a village of Patna district remark that "A kind of political poison has suddenly paralysed village society. People have started hating each other, said Bindeshwari Rai, 50.

The most important trading town of North Bihar, the head quarters of the famous Tirhut division and also the seat of some of the most powerful Bhumihars land owners - politicians of the state besides Begusarai and Mokama is loosing their base due to lack of caste solidarity and other factors.

The table given below show that in both the areas, the candidates, who had won and fought the election, mostly belonged to the dominant caste. In Begusarai, dominant caste dominated the election, the candidate belonging to other castes, had in some cases also won the election.

The table also show that there is no consistency in the percentage of votes secured by the candidates, who have regularly been winning the election. Sometimes, they secure more than 70% votes, while at others the percentage is even less than 40%. What is the reason for these ups and downs? Some question was put forth in both the constituencies to the respondents, to which their reply was, that this was the result of the "wind blowing" in favour of or against the candidate at the particular moment.

In the last Lok Sabha election for 54 seats of Parliament for undivided Bihar, NDA (National Democratic Alliance) bagged 41 seats in which some Bhumihar caste members also won the election. Anand Mohan, a Bhumihar, formed Bihar Peoples' Party. His wife Smt. Lovely Anand won Lok Sabha seat only one's from Bihar. Another local MP (Jehanabad) from Samta Party Arun Kumar, is a Bhumihar. In the 14th Lok Sabha election, some Bhumihar caste politicians fought the election but lost their seats.

It is evident from the above, that the importance of caste plays an important role in selection of

Table - 5

Percentage of vote of different caste candidates of Begusarai Constituency, who have fought and have won the elections from the Ist General Elections to the Last General Election and their parties

Year in which election was held	*Candidates who had fought the Election*	*Caste of the candidates*	*Candidates who had won the Election*	*Percentage of the votes*	*Party of the candidates*
1	2	3	4	5	6
1952	Suraj Pd. Singh	Bhumihar	Suraj Pd.	72.76	Congress
	Yagneswar Pd. Singh	Bhumihar	(Upper Caste)	22.33	Socialist
	Jagati Narain Lal Agarwal	Baniya		17.32	Independent
1957	Suraj Pd. Singh	Bhumihar	Suraj Pd. Singh	26.18	Congress
	Jugal Paswan	S. Caste	(Upper Caste)	21.27	Communist
1962	Ram Narain Chaudhry	Bhumihar	Ram Narain (Upper Caste)	60.3	C.P.I.
	Chandra Shekar Pd.	Bhumihar		6.9	Independent
	Ram Shankar Pd. Sharma	Bhumihar		4.52	Swatantra
	Ganesh Pd. Mehto	S. Caste		3.0	Socialist

Contd...

1967	Bhola Singh	Bhumihar	Bhola Singh (Upper Caste)	62.33	Independent
	R. Chaudhry	Bhumihar		19.60	I.N.C.
	P. Dass	Bengali		10.33	Independent
	R. Singh	Bhumihar		5.34	Independent
1969	B.N. Singh	Bhumihar	Bhola Singh (Upper Caste)	40.46	C.P.I.
	R. P. Singh	Bhumihar		7.94	B.J.S.
	Lakshmi Narain Singh	Bhumihar		2.34	S.S.P.
1972	Bhola Singh	Bhumihar	Bhola Singh (Upper Caste)	34.33	C.P.I
	Gita Singh	Bhumihar		18.47	I.N.C.
1977	Bhola Singh	Bhumihar	Bhola Singh (Upper Caste)	33.99	I.N.C.
	Rameshwar Pd. Singh	Bhumihar		27.01	I.M.P.
	Sukdeo Singh	Bhumihar		8.15	I.N.D.
	Narain Sharma	Bhumihar		7.08	I.N.D.
	Rajendra Singh	Bhumihar		4.26	I.N.D.
1980	Bhola Singh	Bhumihar	Bhola Singh (Upper Caste)	44.16	I.N.C. (I)
	Basudeo Singh	Bhumihar		36.13	C.P.I.
	Chandra Chur Deo	Bhumihar		4.87	B.I.S.
	Ram Narain Mehto	S. Castes		3.04	I.N.P.
	Rameshwar Singh	Bhumihar		1.49	Independent

Sources : Government of India, *Report on the First, Second, Third, Mid-Term, Fourth, Fifth, Sixth, Seventh General Elections in India*, Vol. II and IV (Statistical), Election Commission of India.

candidates by political parties at the time of general elections and also in the pattern of voting.

(b) Peasant Politics

M.N. Srinivas, the well known sociologist, was of the view that the caste system in India is growing more powerful. Modern means of communication, the spread of education and an increase in prosperity have contributed to the strengthening of the caste system, especially through the formation of caste associations, which further boost its organisational capability and on many occa-sions it becomes the conduict for political recruitment.

The story of the nationalist struggle in Bihar is the story of Peasent Movement on whose back constitutionalist politicians rode to power and began their scramble for the loaves and fishes of governance. But peasants in Bihar, as elsewhere, are not one homogeneous, undifferentiated mass : one section of the peasantry struggled upto the time of Zamindari abolition and quite another section is in revolt today, which will be discussed in subsequent paragraphs.

Peasant politics started in Bihar due to social and economic oppression of tenants and sexual exploitation of their womenfolk which was rampant to such an extent, particularly in Masaurha Zamindari that tenants outside Masaurha were unwilling to get their daughters married there. It was from Masurha that the Kisan Sabha, which grew into a formidable peasant force in Bihar, made its beginning in 1928.

(Swami Sahajanand Autobiography: Mera Jewan Sangharsh)

To begin with, the organised Peasant Movement started its journey with a small peasant organisation in 1928 and with the formation of the Patna District Kisan Sabha under the leadership of Swami Sahajanand Saraswati. During 1939 its members increased to 4.0 lakhs, which shows its popularity. Later it developed into the Bihar Provincial Kisan

Sabha and became the core of the All India Kisan Sabha which struggled against Zamindari. After the abolition of Zamindari in the 1950s, although the formal organisation remained extant largely under the control of CPI, it lost its bite.

It also started social reform movement in order to attain an appropriate ritual status but soon it grew into formidable Anti-Zamindari Organisations culminating in the 1930s in the Kisan Sabha. The movement received support from Congressmen, Socialists and the CPI led by the peasant activist, Karyanand Sharma and other radical elements in Bihar politics. However, the Chief Minister. Shri Krishna Sinha who represented both petty zamindari and Bhumihar junker-Kulak interests, was not very enthusiastic in spite of having been one of the founder of the Kisan Sabha. The Kisan Sabha did manage to get zamindari abolished, but the gains accrued to an equally rapacious system of capitalist-agriculture characterised by gun-toting junkers in North Bihar and Harijan-Hunting Kulaks in the South-Central Plains. In the 1970s when the Peasant Movement rose again in the region, albeit on different premises and demands, several rudimentry mass organisations of peasants came up here and there. In the early 1980s, the need was felt to consolidate them into one formation and the Bihar Pradesh Kishan Sabha of Swami Sahajanand even as it took up new issues related primarily to the demands of the small peasants and agricultural labourers, made no heeds towards solving their burning issues.

The movement in Central Bihar is strongest in seven districts: Bhojpur, Rohtas, Patna, Gaya, Jehanabad, Aurangabad and Buxar. The CPI (ML) liberation in the main leading force behind it. This phase of peasant struggle in Bihar had its genesis in the peasant struggle of Bhojpur and Patna between

1922 and 1979. The present phase of peasant struggle began in the rural areas of Patna in the early 1980s and soon spread to Nalanda and Jehanabad. The patronage of the government can be proved from the following incident. On 22nd October 1981, the Bhumi Sena held an open demonstration of about 3,000 people in defiance of the prohibitory orders. They raised the slogans such as "fasal kategi kheton mein, aag laggegi jhopriyon mein", "Naxaliyun ki ek dawai, chhah inch chotta kar do bhai". (The crop will be harvested the fields and fire will engulf the hutments and the only remedy the naxalites is to cut them short by six inches—that is chop their heads). The police was not only escorting this illegal procession but was even distributing pamphlets and raising slogans. This armed procession of landlords at Bikram included Diwakar Sharma and Jaiprakash Singh of Congress (I), Subhas Andhra Singh, Vice-President of the Patna district BJP and Haldeshwar Singh of the CPI. Lok Dal activists were also reported to have been present in the procession.

In the year 1981, four significant events may be identified which fuelled the unrest in the affected areas of Patna. They were: the aftermath of the procession in Bikram on 24th September; the aftermath of the incident of rape in Lahsuna village in September; the arrests in Lahsuna and the incident at Nadwan Railway Station on 3rd October; and the police firing at Narihi Pithi. It should also be noted that despite the oft-repeated charge of violence by armed extremists", they were the only four incidents which the police referred as concrete examples of 'Naxalite violence'.

The coming up of the Bihar Pradesh Kisan Sabha brought all functions of peasants under one banner and also attracted the middle peasants. Hence the caste colour of this movement also started disintegrating. One can confine this by taking examples of some block

(1) Naubatpur

Kripa Narayan Singh was the President of the BPKS of this block. This block is dominated by Bhumihar landlords. The landless and poor peasants and also middle peasants of all castes including Bhumihar protested against the landlord Narendra Sharma of Karhi village and Ved Prakash Singh of Chotikopa village. Both of them are Bhumihars by caste.

(2) Masauri

Arvind Kumar, a Bhumihar is the dominant peasant leader of this block. This block is dominated by Kurmi landlords. In the initial stage Harijans took part in this struggle but later on all sections of peasants started to mobilize themselves against landlords. In Lehsuna, Dr. Chandra Sekhar Singh who was a Kurmi by caste organized the peasants against the Kurmi landlords. In this area Lal Babu Singh was murdered by his own caste Kurmi landlords.

(3) Bikram

It is a Bhumihar dominated area with a majority of the landlords belonging to this caste. At the same time, the leadership of BPKS are in the hands of T.N. Azad, Suresh Singh, Naresh Singh, all of them belongs to Bhumihar caste and are poor peasants.

A new awakening took place in Bhojpur, Aurangabad, Rohtas and parts of Gaya. For protection of agrarian vested interest, political parties of the areas have backed the formation of caste-based private armies or senas in the state. The Bhumihars have their Brahmarshi Sena and Ranveer Sena. Sardar Krishna Singh, then MLA was the chief of Brahmarshi Sena, whereas now the Ranveer Sena is headed by Brahmeshwar Singh. Politician like Ramashray Prasad Singh, Jagdish Sharma, Ramjatan Sinha, R.P. Singh and even Dr. C.P. Thakur have sympathy towards it.

The linkage between national and the peasant movements have been brought out with great clarity by Majid Siddiqi and K.N. Panikkar (from 1920 to 1922-U.P.) "The association of the Kisans with national politics helped both the peasant movements as well as the political movements for they drew sustenance from and gave support to each other at different stages. The movement from below was thus given an initial boost by the cohesion that politics lent to it.

The gender-specific brutality of the Ranveer Sena, a 19th century tale of Ranveer Baba who fought Kharwar Rajputs in the Shahabad area, has been successful revoked to make Bhumihars rally around this sena, setup in Bhojpur's Belaur village in 1994 and operating in Jehanabad district since 1995, is unique. Jehanabad has seen the rise and fall of many private armies over the past two decades, until the advent of the Ranveer Sena. The Ranveer Sena is trying to overrun the Naxalite citadel in Jehanabad after having established a reign of terror in Bhojpur. The Sena began its most ghastly attack in Laxmanpur-Bathe in 1997. In retaliation to this the Maoist Communist Centre has massacred 54 Rajputs and 42 Bhumihars respectively in Dalalchak-Baghaura (1987) and Bara (1992) both outside the Jehanabad theatre of conflict. Similarly attack on Sena activists, supporters and sympathisers in Bhimpura, Usri Bazar and finally in Senari village in Jehanabad district in which 34 Bhumihars were massacred, took place.

Though Senari has proved to be a serious blow, the aspiration of the Sena to demolish the citadel of naxalism in Jehanabad has not died. In all the above activities 'Gohar' is sent. It is a response of a divided society, unmediated by the rule of the state. A Gohar is the ultimate expression of social solidarity, expressed generally in sheer force-of-arms power terms in lawless Bihar.

Besides this, some more aggression took place in which Bhumihars were involved in one way or the others. These are given below.

Place	Aggressor	Victim	issue
1) Baijatpur	Bhumihar (landlord)	Harijan (Agri., Labourers and share croppers)	Wage, Share croppers right over land.
2) Daheya	Yadav (and all classes)	Bhumihar (poor peasants and one big landlord)	Retaliation
3) Jarpa	Bhumihar (Landlord)	Yadav (poor peasants and share croppers)	Land disputes
4) Parasbigha	Bhumihar (Landlord)	Yadav (share cropper)	Share croppers right

The Sena, too, flexed its muscles during the 1999 Lok Sabha election in which it had supported the alliance of BJP and Samata Party and also became the first private Army ever to enter the election fray in Bihar under the banner of the Rashtravadi Kisan Maha-Sangha, its peasant front, it fielded Rang-Bahadur Singh, a Rajput, as its candidate for the Arrah Seat, and also garnered an impressive 12.8% votes. At present, Brahmeshwar Singh, now in jail and founding commander of Ranveer Sena has announced his candidature from Arrah Lok Sabha Constituency (2004). He lost this seat to the RJD Mrs. Kanti Singh.

The Ranveer Sena, according to the massliners, represents the last desperate course of upper caste landlords struggle to retain the old socio-economic order. The massliners see their struggle as a continuation of a three-decade-long process of challenging the existing order which began in 1967 and which has considerably demolished the old order and changed and reformatted the balance of power in rural society.

To sum up, we encounter in Bihar the phenomenon of a gradually enlarging circle of political competition. In the initial stages, the political scene was dominated by one or two castes, namely, Bhumihars and Kayasthas. As political awareness grew and hitherto politically immobile caste groups realised the importance of politics as an instrument of satisfying mobility aspirations, the domination of upper caste came to be challenged. This in turn led to defensive and counter-alliances and it activated and assimilated other castes groups in the political arena which we faced now-a-days.

(c) Independence Movement

During 1760-70 some of the Bihar zamindars discontented with the company rose against it and espoused the cause of Chait Singh. Similarly after treaty of 21 January, 1798, Wazir Ali was sent to Banaras to live there as a pensioner. Discontented with his lot, he planned an All India Conspiracy against the British and had some confederates in Bihar including Raja Mitrajit Singh of Tekari. During Babu Kunwar Singh revolt against Britishers, many Bhumihars of Shahabad and Arrah took his side. During Ranchi and Doranda march of insurgents several people allied with them such as Thakur Biswanath Sahi of Barkargarh and Pandey Ganpat Rai of Bhorno were the leading supporters of the rebels. Besides (Ramgarh Conference) Shukla, and Swami Sahajanand some of the patriotic Leaders of Bihar worked at Champaran under the guidance of Mahatma

Gandhi and Sri Krishna Sinha was one of them. During civil disobedience for complete independence (1930-34), a regular camp of volunteers was started at Bihpur in the Bhagalpur districts. Similarly in Munger district, Congress activists were increasingly under the leadership of Srikrishna Sinha was arrested for breaking salt law. In Congress ministry, formed on 20 July, 1937, Sri Krishna Sinha became Chief Minister, whereas Ram Dayalu Singh became Speaker.

In the present political scenario, large landless castes now have the power of voting strength, so they may and sometimes do challenge the traditionally-dominant caste which has power derived from land control. Dominant caste as well as ascendant castes are usually tied in with the important political parties of a region, and upward mobility through the political party organization takes place. The most talented men desert the village political arenas for the larger arenas at district, state, and national levels. Sometimes local rivalries are projected onto wider stages. Within localities, elected leaders often displace the hereditary caste headmen and other traditional leaders in the performance of such duties as the settlement of disputes, leadership in village ceremonial events, and other undertakings are taking place and Bhumihar is no exception to it.

References

- Andre Beteille; 'Caste, Class and Power; Berkelay, University of California Press, 1969.
- Arvind N. Das; "The Republics of Bihar", Penguin Books India (P) Ltd., 1992.
- Rajni Kothari (Ed.); Caste in Indian Politics, Orient Longman Ltd; 1970.
- S. Akinchan; "Caste, Class and Politics", Gyan Publishing House, New Delhi, 1995.

5

Caste and Education

There is a direct relationship between caste and education. As B.B. Mishra puts it: "The new forces which weakened the traditional economic order were those of western education and a capitalist economy, a free judiciary and parliamentary institutions. The contribution of western education lay mainly in three things. Firstly, it broke the intellectual monopoly of the Brahmins by opening the doors of education to all classes. Secondly, it created an educated class of Indians comprising members of the various learned professions who cut across caste and became supporters of liberal reforms. Thirdly, it set in motion an unprecedented degree of occupational mobility which helped to increase social mobility.

It is not an accident that the division of Bihar universities as 'spheres of influence' among caste groups took place, but other factors were also playing their respective roles in shaping it as for, example Patna for Kayasthas, Magadh (Gaya) for the Rajputs, Bihar (Muzaffarpur) for the Bhumihars and Mithila

(Darbhanga) for the Maithil Brahmins - has now become an old story. The name of the game is not distribution of patronage alone in the 'ed biz' any longer but the sale, with profit, of the commodities of education. Gandhiji, on his way to Champaran to perform his first Satyagraha in India, stayed at the 'Grierson Bhumihar Brahmin College' (the present Langat Singh College, Muzaffarpur), and this label of importance has its contribution in increasing the popularity of the College.

From the days of Swami Sahajanand Saraswati, who had special affection with Bihta; a sankrit school was opened in the premise of Bihta Ashram to educate all, especially, the children from Bhumihar caste. Now-a-days many other educational institutions in his name has been opened in different parts of the state, (including Jharkhand), i.e., at Ranchi, Bokaro, Patna, Swami Sahajanand Saraswati Kisan Bhawan at Muzaffarpur, etc.; Similarly, the contribution in the field of education by Sir Ganesh Dutt, can not be forgottan, on whose name Sir Ganesh Dutt Inter College and School at Patna is working and providing education to all sections of society, Ram Dayalu Babu had done same thing at Muzaffarpur, Sh. Murarilal Tyagi established school at Keshavpuram, New Delhi. Sh. Kapildeo Singh also contributed a lot towards upliftment of Bhumihar caste in this field. Another name in the field of education is Prof. Thakur Prasad Singh; Besides this the Brahmarshi Samaj is also running "Society for Social Health Care" with it head office at Patna. Over and above the first chief Minister of Bihar, Sh. S.K. Sinha was himself a great social worker and educationist and on whose name many institutions are functioning in different parts of the state and contributing a lot for the well being of common people.

Once a famous library in Naubatpur Block (Patna district) in which many old manuscripts and books were kept and now in a dialipidated condition, was also started by a prominent Bhumihar family of the area.

When new opportunities in various walks of life were created as a result of contact with the outside world, it was usually the upper castes which took advantage of these opportunities. Thus the existing inequalities were cumulated. Take, for example, the utilisation of newly created opportunities by different castes. The 1931 census for Bihar and Orissa reveals that of the four upper castes, the Kayasthas have been the most literate caste (372 literates per 1,000), followed by the Brahmins (195 literates per 1,000) the Bhumihars (136 literates per 1,000) and the Rajputs (120 literates per 1,000). The table given on page 109 shows the caste and education in Bihar.

The said table indicates that a large majority of students came from the four upper castes, 70.0 percent in 1936, 67.74 percent in 1943, 73.16 percent in 1948, 87.23 percent in 1953, 65.61 percent in 1958 and 62.68 percent in 1963. The position of Bhumihar students in respect of the above is low i.e., in 1936-20.0 percent, in 1953-25.53 percent, in 1958-14.06 percent and in 1963-25.37 percent.

A small decline in the number of upper castes students is constrasted with the slow but steady rise in the number of students coming from other castes. This gradual rise in the number of students from the 'dispossessed' sections of Bihar society reflects a change taking place in the stratification system, and presumably points to the growing appreciation among under-privileged groups for education as an instrument of status aspirations. Upper castes still dominate the field of education however, and to this extent maintain the process of cumulative inequality.

Table : Caste and Education in Bihar :
Admission to B.A. Classes in Patna College, 1936-1963*

Castes	1936 N=30	1943 N=34	1948 N=41	1953 N=47	1958 N=64	1963 N=67
Brahmins	10.00	20.59	26.83	29.79	23.43	11.94
Bhumihar Brahmins	20.00	5.88	17.07	25.53	14.06	25.37
Rajputs	10.00	5.88	9.75	8.51	12.50	7.46
Kayasthas	30.00	35.29	19.51	23.40	15.62	17.91
Sub-total	**70.00**	**67.64**	**73.16**	**87.23**	**65.61**	**62.68**
Other Castes	6.66	11.76	7.31	6.38	26.56	25.38
Muslims	23.33	20.59	19.51	6.38	7.82	11.94
Total	99.99	99.99	99.99	99.99	99.99	100.00

* Source : Office of the Patna College, Patna. The table is based on a twenty percent random sample.

Table. Caste and Education of Active Members in 4 Districts of Bihar, 1961 (in per cent)

District	Castes	Literate	Middle School	High School	Inter-mediate	Graduate	Post-Graduate	Law	Tradi-tional	Total
1	2	3	4	5	6	7	8	9	10	11
Saharsha	Brahmin	—	3.85	3.84	1.28	—	—	—	15.38	
N=78	Bhumihar Brahmin	—	1.28	—	—	—	1.28	—	—	2.56
	Rajput	3.85	8.98	3.85	1.28	—	—	2.56	1.28	21.80
	Kayastha	—	2.56	1.29	—	2.56	—	—	—	6.41
	Lower Castes	1.28	1.28	7.69	2.56	3.85	3.85	1.28	1.28	23.07
	Scheduled Castes	1.28	8.98	2.56	2.56	1.28	—	—	1.28	17.94
	Muslims	—	—	1.28	—	—	—	—	1.28	2.56
	Total	6.41	29.93	23.08	10.24	8.97	5.13	3.84	5.12	89.72
Saran	Brahmin	—	3.29	1.31	1.31	0.67	0.67	1.31	3.94	12.50
N=152	Bhumihar Brahmin	—	3.94	1.97	1.97	1.97	1.32	3.30	—	14.47
	Rajput	0.67	7.23	3.29	3.29	1.97	1.97	1.97	1.97	0.67
19.74										
	Kayastha	—	—	—	1.31	0.66	0.66	—	—	2.63
	Lower Castes	0.67	5.92	3.94	2.62	3.29	3.29	1.31	0.67	21.71
	Scheduled Castes	—	3.93	0.67	—	—	—	0.67	—	5.27
	Muslims	0.66	0.66	0.66	1.32	—	—	3.29	—	5.27
	Total	2.00	24.97	11.84	10.50	8.56	7.91	11.85	5.28	82.91

1	2	3	4	5	6	7	8	9	10	11
Darbhanga	Brahmin	0.82	5.74	4.10	2.87	2.05	2.05	5.74	3.68	27.05
N=244	Bhumihar Brahmin	—	1.23	0.82	1.23	0.82	0.82	—	1.23	6.15
	Rajput	0.82	5.33	2.87	1.64	1.64	1.23	3.28	2.87	19.68
	Kayastha	0.41	0.41	0.82	0.40	—	0.41	0.41	1.23	4.09
	Lower Castes	—	3.69	3.69	0.82	3.28	0.41	1.63	0.82	14.34
	Scheduled Castes	1.23	4.91	2.06	1.64	0.82	0.41	—	0.41	11.48
	Muslims	—	—	1.23	1.64	2.05	—	1.23	1.23	7.38
	Total	3.38	21.31	15.59	10.24	10.66	5.33	12.29	11.47	90.17
Shahabad	Brahmin	—	5.25	6.28	2.62	2.09	1.04	1.57	2.62	21.47
N = 191	Bhumihar Brahmin	—	2.09	2.09	—	1.04	1.58	—	0.53	7.33
	Rajput	0.53	5.23	3.66	0.53	1.58	2.09	3.13	1.04	17.79
	Kayastha	—	1.57	3.16	0.53	0.52	—	1.04	0.53	7.33
	Lower Castes	1.57	3.65	5.72	1.04	0.53	1.04	2.10	1.04	16.69
	Scheduled castes	0.53	4.17	1.04	—	—	—	0.53	0.53	6.80
	Muslims	—	0.52	0.52	0.52	0.53	0.53	—	—	2.62
	Total	2.63	22.48	22.47	5.23	6.29	6.28	8.37	6.28	80.03

* Other minor castes and cases not known have been left out.

In similar way the table given above shows the relationship between caste and education of the active members (political) in four districts of undivided Bihar, in the year 1961 (in percent) :-

If we analyse the above table, the following points come out :-

In Saharsha district, the total literates were 6.41 percent, middle pass 29.93 percent, in high school 23.08 percent, intermediate - 10.24 percent, graduate- 8.97 percent, post-graduate- 5.13 percent, law-3.84 percent and in traditional education - 5.12 percent out of which the percentage of Bhumihar Brahmin active members were the following :- literate - nil, middle pass - 1.28 percent, high school, intermediate and graduate – nil, post-graduate- 1.28 percent and others- nil. In Saran district out of total literate of 2.00 percent, Bhumihars were nil, middle pass 24.97 percent (Bhumihar - 3.94 percent), high school 11.84 percent (Bhumihar - 1.97 percent), intermediate 10.50 percent (Bhumihar - 1.97 percent), graduate 8.56 percent (Bhumihar-1.97 percent), post graduate 7.91 percent (1.32 percent Bhumihar), Law-11.85 percent (Bhumihar - 3.30 percent), traditional 5.28 percent (Bhumihar-nil).

In Darbhanga out of total literate of 3.38 percent (Bhumihar-Nil), middle pass - 21.31 percent (Bhumihar-1.23 percent), high school-15.59 percent (Bhumihar-0.82 percent), intermediate-10.24 percent (Bhumihar - 1.23 percent), graduate- 10.66 percent (Bhumihar-0.82 percent), post graduate - 5.33 percent (Bhumihar-0.82 percent), law- 12.29 percent (Bhumihar-nil) and in traditional Education-11.47 percent (Bhumihar-1.23 percent). In Shahabad out of total literate of 2.63 (Bhumihar-nil), middle pass 22.48 percent (Bhumihar-2.09 percent high school - 22.47 percent (Bhumihar-2.09 percent) inter-mediate 5.23 percent (Bhumihar-nil), graduate 6.29 percent (Bhumihar-1.04% post-graduate - 6.28 percent

(Bhumihar-1.58 percent), law-8.37 percent (Bhumihar-nil), traditional education- 6.28 percent (Bhumihar-0.53 percent).

Another remarkable fact is that in respect of other political representatives upper castes, Bhumihars were the lowest educated, i.e., 2.56 percent in all in Saharsha district. In Saran district it was ahead of Brahmin and Kayastha, i.e., total 14.47 percent. In Darbhanga district again it was ahead only of Kayastha, i.e., total 6.15 percent literate. And in Shahabad district total literary of both Kayasthas and Bhumihars were 7.33 percent each which were again the lowest literary compared to Brahmin, i.e., 21.47 percent and Rajputs, i.e., 17.79 percent.

All these facts indicates that the education was at the lowest in the political representatives among this caste, In some other districts the situation was better than this. This may be due to little or no awareness regarding the benefits of education, because Bhumihars were the late starter after bifurcation of the Bihar State when they felt the need of education to grab government posts in different departments and they began to educate themselves. In recent years, the situation has already changed and most of the political representatives of Bhumihars are educated well and some have even earned reputation in their respective field of vocation, as to name; Dr. C.P. Thakur, who was a Minister in Central Government; is also a well known doctor in his hometown Constituency.

Despite low educational profile of Bhumihar in the 60's, due to its higher social status, economic well being and political dominance, they reaped the political benefits. They enjoyed political power because of their dominance in very crucial areas of social, ritual and economic systems. But now their attitude has changed and they are providing their children best available education to reap its benefit. Besides urbanities now even agriculturists children with rural backgrounds are competing in most of the competitive exams and holding posts of importance in central as well as state government.

The latest development in the field of education in Bihar is that education mafias have come up and to counteract it Bhumihars have also opened many schools and are not lagging behind in this field. These schools are running successfully in whole of the state.

References

- Das, Arvind N., the Republic of Bihar.
- Caste in Education; Eastern Economist, vol. 39, october 5, 1962.
- Brahmarshi Samaj journal (Quarterly) Jan-March' 2003.

6

Bhumihars and The Kisan Sabha

The Bhumihars are also a caste of agriculturists but there is greater differentiation within the caste itself than among the Yadavas with whom in August, 1926 the relationship became very strained at Barh and later on this tension increased; but the government; didnot heeded against it earnestly. There were also some big landlords family (e.g., Sir Ganesh Dutt) belonging to this caste, but most of the Bhumihars constituted the sub-stantial tenantry, which in economic term, would constitute a section of the upper-middle and rich peasants. In the social scale, Bhumihars were not given the ritual status of Brahmin because they were cultivators. They were denied the right of performing sacrifices to the gods. The major organisational forum of the Bhumihars to deliberate this issue was the "Bhumihar Brahmin Mahasabha." Through meetings and propaganda, attempt were made to prove that the Bhumihars were indeed Brahmins. An important activist in this field was Swami Parmanand Saraswati, a Bhumihar, turned Sanyasi. It was he who got a young Dandi Sanyaṣi named Swami Sahajanand Saraswati involved in the Bhumihar Mahasabha. He investigated into ancient scriptures and carried out a socio-cultural survey of the Bhumihars in different parts of Bihar and U.P., and thus encouraged the Bhumihars to performs all rituals performed by Brahmins. In the tenants lands of Bihar, where their condition was very pitiable, the seeds of the Kisan Sabha was sown. All these facts mentioned above speaks of a long drawn struggle this caste had to face for its survival and to raise its status and in this process a bond was established between Kisan Sabha and this caste. Some important peasant leaders who belongs to this caste and was associated with Kisan Sabha, has been discussed briefly in the subsequent paragraphs.

The foremost leaders of the peasantary in Bihar was, of course, Swami Sahajanand Saraswati. He was born in Ghazipur district in Eastern U.P., in 1889, to a family of Jujautia Brahmins. His mother died when he was a child and Navrang Rai was brought up by his aunt. His father Beni Rai was primarily a cultivator. He went to German Mission High School for study. Later on his family married him to a child bride who died in 1905 or early 1906. In 1907 Navrang Rai was initiated into holy order and took the name Swami Sahajanand Saraswati. He consistently seek census, and indeed change, whether on behalf of the Bhumihars, the Congress or the Peasants. In each instance his conviction and dedication was intense, but in his demand for change on behalf of the peasants of Bihar he came out at his strongest. Earth quake of 1934 in Bihar and Gandhiji apathy towards it led Swami Sahajanand seperation from him. He first joined hands with the congress socialists for the formation of the All India Kisan Sabha.

Such was Swami Sahajanand Saraswati, the charismatic Sanyasi rebel, who laid the foundation of Kisan Organisation in Bihar, built it up into a massive movement, spread it to other parts of India and radicalised it to such an extent that what had started off as a model to bring about reform in the zamindari system, ended up by destroying the system itself. Swami Sahajanand could not, however, witness the legal death of zamindari in Bihar. While the battle for this was still being fought in the legislative and the courts, he passed away on 26th June, 1950.

Although none of the other Kisan Leaders of Bihar had the charismatic hold which Swami Sahajanand did, there were at least three others who in their own ways were also interesting personalities and contributed substantially in making the peasant movement of Bihar into a strong force. Foremost among them and closest to Swami Sahajanand was Pandit Yadunandan Sharma.

Pandit Sharma was born in Majhiawa village in Gaya district in the year 1896, which was a part of Tekari zamindari. He matriculated in 1919 from Tekari High School and did his B.A., in 1929 and participated in the Satyagraha. He was arrested in 1930 and after being released from jail, he joined the Kisan struggle in 1933 and led the famous Sandaka and Rewra movement in the 1930s. In this process he became the indisputed leader of the peasants in Gaya district. After the war (1942), Yadunandan Sharma led the movement for abolition of zamindari. He died in 1975 as a lonely man who after achieving one mission had not been able to move on to the next.

Another leader of the Kisan Sabha who continued the peasant movement even after the abolition of zamindari and continued to remain a powerful figure in the politics of Bihar till 1960s, was

Karyanand Sharma. He was born in 1901 in Sahoor village in Munger district in a poor tenant Bhumihar family. Although he started education in 1906, he had to soon leave the school and help his family in cultivation. However, between 1914 and 1920, he educated himself and matriculated in 1920 just in time for joining the non-Cooperation Movement. In 1927 he organised struggle for peasant, and carried out despite not getting help from other sections. Nevertheless, because of the unity among the tenants, the zamindars had to bow down and this victory became a great morale-booster for the peasants in Munger. In 1935 he was elected secretary of the District Kisan Sabha at its session held at Jamui and again started leading the peasants against zamindari oppression. After the famous Barahiya Bakasht struggle in 1937-39 strictures were passed against him, and in 1938 arrested by the then Congress Government. After his release from jail he rejoined the Kisan Movement and was repeatedly jailed for his this act. Although zamindari was abolished through legislative action after independance, the expolitation of the peasantry remained under the leadership of Karyanand Sharma. The Bihar unit of the CPI waged valiant struggle, and the most notable among them being the *Sathi farms Struggle in Champaran. Before his death Karyanand tried to give peasant movement right direction and increasingly devoted more and more time to the newly formed CPI led Khet Mazdoor Sabha rather than the Kisan Sabha.

In this series the last personality is Rahul

Note* The Sathi struggle was against the Congress. Substantial portion of land alloted to Rampal Sahi and his brother Ram Rekha Prasad Sahi who got about 350 acres of the Sathi farm land. They were related to M.P. Sinha. The settlement with the Shahis were made on 1 November, 1946 ignoring the claims of local people. This took the form of agitation between peasants and Congress supporting Shahis.

Sankrityayana who had a chequered life, changing not only his area of activity but even his name several times. He was born in 1893 in Pandaha village of Azamgarh district in U.P. and was named Kedarnath Pandey. An exceptionally bright student, but he left school. He got-married in 1904. He ran away from home in 1907 and travelled to Calcutta. In 1912 he renounced the world and became a Sadhu, adopting the name of Baba Ramodar Das. He followed different faith and ultimately he met various Buddhist monks during 1915-1918. His way into politics was through non-Cooperation Movement. He also tried to form a Kisan Sabha in 1922 at the Sonepur Mela but as he himself wrote later "The effort was premature". When Kisan Sabha was formed by Swami Sahajanand, he joined it enthusiastically and took part in various peasant agitation. The most notable among these was the "Amwari Satyagraha in Chapra in 1939. In 1940, he became the President of the Bihar Provincial Kisan Sabha. In the same year, he was arrested (15th March). Later on he joined the CPI in 1955. After that he cut himself off from mass movements and engrossed himself in literary and scholastic pursuits. Rahul died on 14 April, 1963, an acknowledged scholar of languages and linguistic and a recognised authority on Central Asia. In his book 'Geography of Saran', he had written that all Bhumihars are Brahmins.

While these four leaders of the Kisan Sabha in Bihar were particularly colourful personalities, there were many others who were equally important at different phases of the movement.

References

- Saraswati, Swami Sahajanand "Bhumihar Brahman Parichaya, Banaras, 1916.
- Ibid., Brahman Samaj Ki Sthithi, Banaras.
- Das, Arvind N., Agrarian Unrest and Socio-Economic Change (1900-1980).

7

Brahmarshi Samaj in India

Castes akin to Bhumihar and known by different names are spread all over the country but the binding ties to all of them are one and that is they belong to one Brahmarshi Samaj. Descriptions of some such castes are given below to understand this Samaj in a better way :-

1. Taga/ Tyagi

An important-cultivating and land-owning caste confined almost altogether to the Upper Ganges-Jamuna Doab and Rohilkhand. They are divided into a Hindu and Mohammadan branch.

The Tyagi claim to be of Brahmanical origin as Sir H.M. Eliot writes "They state that they were invited from Bengal to these parts by Raja Janamejaya for the purpose of exterminating snakes; which fable, though sufficiently ridiculous in itself, no doubt veils under an allegorical type, a most important-historical fact. It is also mentioned in the "Adi Parva" of the Mahabharata. It was for the purpose of officiating at this serpent sacrifice that Janamejaya is said to have invited Brahmans from Gaur. After performing the rituals, they were remunerated, which some rejected and others received in the shape of land, on account of which they were called Tagas/Tyagi from having consented to relinquishment (*tyag*) of their creed as Brahmans by pursuing agriculture which they are forbidden by the *shastras* to practice.

Tyagi resides in Uttar Pradesh, Haryana and Delhi. Crooke (1896) says that on the whole it seems not unreasonable to believe that, like the Bhumihar Brahman of the eastern part of the province, the Tyagi may have been originally Gaur Brahmans, who lost status by abandoning priestly functions for taking to agriculture. According to a legend, when Parashuram killed Kshetriyas, the land so begotten was given to Brahmans who started cultivating it. The total population of Tyagi/Taga, according to the 1931 census was 137,598. They were predominantly found in the United Provinces. Cultivation is their main economic activity.

In Uttar Pradesh, the Taga/Tyagi are concentrated in the Bulandshahr, Moradabad, Muzaffarnagar, Meerut, Ghaziabad, Saharanpur, and Bijnore districts. Their mother tongue is Hindi and it is also used for intergroup communication. The Devnagri script is used. Tyagi is their surname. According to the 1931 census, the population of the Taga in the United Provinces of Agra and Oudh was 133,153. They are vegetarian. Wheat, rice, and maize are their staple cereals. Men take alcoholic drinks occasionally.

The Tagas have two subdivisions, namely Dasa or Daswan and Bisa or Biswan. The former allow widow remarriage while the latter prohibit it. If a Bisa allows and approves widow remarriage he at once falls into the Dasa sub division. The Dasa and Bisa form two endogamous groups and within these groups they have various gotras, such as, Vishwamitra, Vashistha and Bhardwaja. Crooke (1896) has also recorded two main sub divisions, Dasa/Daswan and Bisa/Biswan among them. The Tagas were further stratified into several sections, like Bachhae, Bias, Bargala, Chauhan, Chandel, Dikshit, Gaur, Sanadh and Vasisth. Male equigeniture is the inheritance rule followed by the community, and succession is by the eldest male member of the family. They observe birth pollution, name giving ceremony, tonsure (mundan), thread-wearing ceremony and first feeding of cereals (annaprashan). The marriage rituals are performed at the bride's residence and circumambulation (phera or saptapadi) is the main ritual connected with it. They bury their dead and observe pollution for thirteen days. Ashes and bones (*phul*) are collected and disposed of on the third day after cremation. Land is the main resource which is controlled by individual ownership. They are settled cultivators since time immemorial. Business and government or private services are the other means of livelihood. They are Hindu, and considerable number of them are affiliated to pirs, individually or as a family.

The Taga in Haryana are better known as Tyagi/ Tyagi Brahman. They have a Brahmanical origin but they left their traditional occupation of *puja-path* and has taken up agriculture. They are concentrated in the Sonipat and Karnal districts of the state. They use the Haryanvi and Devanagri Script for both inter and intra group communication. Many of them are conversant with Hindi also. They are vegetarian but a few among them have started taking eggs and meat. The younger generation has also started taking alcoholic drinks. Rose (1919) states that there is only one sub divisions, namely Badha amongst the Taga inhabiting Jamuna Khaderi, Karnal, Haryaa, Jind and Sirsa.

Property is divided equally among sons only.

Succession right is transcended to the eldest son. After birth, pollution (*Sootak*) is observed for thirteen to forty days. Rituals observed are naming ceremony, annaprashan and thread-wearing ceremony (*janeu*). The marriage rituals are performed at the bridegroom's residence and they include Dekhna, Sagai, Barat, Phere, and Bidai. Baithana or Chadar pana is permissible. An avoidance relationship is observed between daughter and father-in-law. Joking relationship is also observed. Inter-family links are cordial. Dead are cremated and pollution is observed for seventeen days. Annual *shradh* are observed in the memory of dead elders. However, the communication as a whole is stratified into several exogamous gotra like Bhardwaja, Parashar, Dikshit, and Bachas Vasisth. These are the same as reported for other Brahman communities. The Gotras indicates descent and regulate marriage alliances. Rose (ibid.) has also found existence of similar gotras. Either Tyagi or *gotras* names are used as surnames. Agriculture is the main occupation of the community. Land resources is controlled by the individual families. They are also in private and government service too. Now-a-days some have become followers of the Arya-Samaj sect.

The Tyagi of Delhi claim that they were Gaur Brahman at one time. They are distributed in both rural and urban areas of the union territory. They converse in hindi and communicate in the devanagri script within the family and kin group and also with others. They are vegetarian but donot take masurdal, onion and garlic. However, tendency to consume non-vegetarian food has been observed. Wheat and rice constitute their staple cereals. Alcoholic drinks purchased from the market are occasionally consumed by men.

The Taga/Tyagi community has two subgroups, Bade Tyagi and Chottey or Chotteyor or Dassa Tyagi. Each subgroups has a number of *gotras* namely

Bhardwaja, Teetwal, Bhasyan, Vasisth, Sangla, Sandilya, Kashyap, Gaur, Gautam, etc. They use Tyagi or gotras as surnames. As the name implies, the Bade Tyagi claim higher status in social hierarchy. The subgroups and gotras regulate marital alliances and also indicate descent. Naming and tonsure (mundan) ceremonies are observed both for male and female children, whereas the thread-wearing ceremony is observed for male children only. They cremate the dead and observe death pollution ceremony.

In Delhi majority of them have given up their traditional occupation because their agricultural land has been acquired by the Delhi Development Authority. They are now engaged in various other occupations and trade and in industry. Some of them are in government jobs and private jobs. Traditionally, they donot accept food from lower castes, but they accept it from and exchange the same with the Gujjar, Agri, Reya, Ahir, Bania, Brahman, Rajput, Khatri, Kayastha and some other communities.

Tyagi, are endogamous groups in general and follow the rules of Brahmanical exogamy. Polyandry and sexual license before marriage are strictly prohibited. Polygamy is allowed only when the first wife is barren. The age for marriage was from eight to fifteen during British period. There is no legalised divorce. There is no bride-price; but it is usual to give dowry with the bride. At present the above norms or customs are not followed strictly by the Tyagis.

The Taga follow Hinduism and worship all Hindu gods and goddesses. A few of them have embraced have Islam and given up the pre.- change practices They have great reverence for Bhoomiya devta - sacred places commonly visited by them are Gurgaonwali Mata and Garh Ganga. Taga celebrate all Hindu festivals. These festivals are of socio-religious significance. Folklore, folk-tales and folk songs also exist. These are used on different occasions.

They worship Mahadeva and are very careful to propitiate the sainted dead of the household. One way of appeasing the spirit of the dead man is to make an unmarried boy drink milk under a *pipal* tree on the death day in every fortnight for a year and then on each succeeding anniversary.

Distribution of Tyagi according to 1891 Census in U.P.

District	Number
Dehradun	12
Saharanpur	15,961
Muzaffarnagar	12,792
Meerut	43,290
Bulandshahr	6,588
Bijnor	10,952
Budaun	21
Moradabad	9,822
Shahjanpur	1
Tarai	49
Hardoi	1

(2) Chitpavan

This caste numbering 113,605 (males 58,150, females 55,455) at the Census of 1901, and 119, 611 (M-62, 447, F-57, 164) at the Census of 1931 are found in all parts of the Deccan, Goa and Konkan. They are also known as Chitpols, Chiplunas and Konkanasths. The name Chitpavan, Chitpol and Chipluna appears to come from the town of Chiplun in Ratnagiri, their original and chief settlement, the old name of which is said to have been Chitpolan. They began to call themselves Konkanasths about 1715 AD. When Peshwa Balaji Vishwanath rose to the importance in the Maratha Kingdom. Their worship of Parashuram, the slayer of the Kshetriya and the coloniser of the Konkan on Parashuram hill close to Chiplun, the fact that they are called Parashuram shrishti or Parashuram's creation. The meaning of Chitpavan is 'pure from the pyre', which the sound of their name suggests to some extent explain the curious legends of which they are the subjects. According to Sahyadri Khand, Parashuram purified the corpses by burning them on a funeral pyre or chita and also rewarded his new priests by granting areas in that region. So, the name became Chitpavans and their settlement Chitpolan. At the same time, it seems probable that the Chitpavans like the bulk of Konkan Brahman, did not enter the Konkan by land. Their fair complexion, the extent to which they use the Konkan dialect in their homes, and the legend of their arrival as shipwrecked sailors seem to show that they came into the south Konkan from beyond the sea. Whether they were foreigners is doubtful. The legend of the shipwrecked sailors being foreigners or malenchhas is to some extent supported by the low position which the Chitpavans formerly held among Brahmans and by the commonness among them of the light or grey eyes. The Chitpavans have a tradition that they came from Amba Jogai in the Nizam's country about 100 miles north of Sholapur. They say that they were originally Deshasth and that fourteen Brahmans of different family-stocks accompanied Parashuram to the Konkan and settled at Chiplun. Until the rise of Balaji Vishwanath Peshwa, who belonged to this class, the Chitpavans held a low position and were known chiefly as spies or harkaras. Even after several generation of power and wealth with strict attention to Brahman rules, the purer classes of Brahmans refused to eat with them and it is said that when Bajirao, the last Peshwa (1796-1818) was at Nasik he was not allowed to go down to the water by the same flight of steps as the priests. Whatever disqualifications may be in theory attach to the Chitpavans, their present social and religious position is as high as that of the Karhade or any other branch of Deccan Brahmans.

Chitpavans are generally fair, well-made and handsome with greenish grey eyes. The women are small and good-looking but many of them are delicate and weak-eyed. In the Konkan in their homes they use a peculiar dialect in many respects not easily followed by Marathi speaking Deccan Hindus. This dialect is fast dying out, and in the Deccan it is known to but few.

The surnames among them as collected by Chapekar numbers 360. There are only fourteen '*gotras*' among them shared by these surnames. The '*gotras*' along with the number of surnames which have them, so thoughtfully listed by Chapekar, are given in the table that follows.

It is believed, on some evidence which is of course not unimpeachable, that the Chitpavans had only sixty surnames among them. Their distribution '*gotra*'-wise is presented in the third column of the table. They are listed in the late *Skandapurana*. That was perhaps ten centuries ago and it is possible that the immigrant Brahmins who became known as the Chitpavans came in a batch of sixty families. Today Chapekar tells us that though he has been able to trace '*gotra*' wise only 360 surnames there are over 400 surnames among the Chitpavans.

Caste, Sub-Caste and Kin

Gotra	No. of contemporary surnames	No. of surnames (old. early or original)
1. Atri	16	3
2. Babhravya	2	2
3. Bharadvaja	20	6
4. Gargya	32	5

Contd...

5. Jamadagnya	4	2
6. Kapi	26	4
7. Kashyapa	46	5
8. Kaundinya	7	2
9. Kaushika	42	5
10. Nityundana	7	2
11. Shandilya	66	7
12. Vasisntha	61	12
13. Vatsa	22	1
14. Vishnuvriddha	9	4

Surnames only tell us the lineages but they cannot by themselves reveal the number of families bearing that lineage name and we cannot form any legitimate conclusion about the relative numbers of people having the different '*gotras*'. We cannot, therefore, use the data for anything like a quantitative assessment of the nature and extent of caste integration that can be and was being brought about through 'gotra'-exogamy and 'gotra'-exogamy-based kinship.

The increase in the surnames cannot be due to infiltration or incorporation of new elements from outside the original group, i.e., the Chitpavan caste, unless we can show, or choose to believe, that the sixty families came at a time when castes were not in existence. As we have attempted to show, and we think with very sound reasons and on strong grounds, that the caste system in a distinctly recognisable form, or of an image not much different from the later system in its fundamental features, must have existed before the seventh century B.C., we have also suggested that 'gotra'-organization had come into existence not later than the sixth or the seventh century B.C. There is no evidence, that the Chitpavans acquired their Gotras in Maharashtra. As a matter of fact we have to start with the assumption that a

Brahmin, wherever south or east, found in India, went there with the 'gotra' and therefore could not have proceeded there much before 600 B.C.

The surnames were in reality only fifty-nine though the Gotras were fourteen, as one of the surnames figured under two 'gotras'. The situation is much more complicated than what one would be led to think to be the case from Chapekar's statement that making allowance for the repetition of certain surnames in more than one 'gotra' the total lineages are 304. For as he has pointed out in the case of the 'Kaushika gotra', out of the 42 listed surnames under that '*gotra*' at least twenty-five have no living representatives.

We can speak of the qualitative aspect of exogamic integration, only if we keep in mind always that aspect is not a complete picture even in rough outline and that the restrictions on the score of prohibited degrees or 'sapinda'-exogamy may modify it, in terms of the number of surnames open for intermarriage.

Among the Chitpavans, as among most of the Brahmins in other parts of India, a person cannot marry one whose father's '*gotra*' is the same as one's own, i.e., as one's own father's. The sixty-six surnames of the '*Shandilya gotra*' of course must seek their mates from outside the sixty-six surnames. As the '*Kashyapa gotra*' is listed in the authoritative texts on the subject to be the '*gotra*'-complex under which '*Shandilya*' is placed they cannot marry anyone of the '*Kashyapa*' *gotra* too. They have, therefore, to eschew in addition, the forty-six surnames of the '*Kashyapa gotra*'. Thus the '*gotra*'-based exogamic rules keep open for inter-marriage to the sixty-six '*Shandilya gotra*' and the forty-six '*Kashyapa gotra*' surnames only two hundred forty-eight out of the total of three hundred and sixty surnames. For the thirty-two surnames of the *'Gargya'-gotra* over and above their thirty-two, the twenty-six surnames of the *'Kapi'-gotra* and the twenty surnames of the *'Bharadvaja'-gotra* being the *'gotra'*-complex under which are listed both the *'Gargya'* and 'Kapi' *gotras*. The surnames of the 'Vishnuvriddha' and 'Nityundana' gotras, nine and seven respectively, can marry out of these sixteen surnames into anyone of the remaining three hundred forty-four surnames. Such are the potentialities of intra-caste integration under the *'gotra'*-exogamy among the Chitpavans.

Chitpavans are either Apasthambas or Rigvedis and belong to the smart sect. They are followers of Shankaracharya. Their family goddess is Jogai or Jogeshwari. Unlike most castes of the Deccan a Chitpavan is not allowed to marry his maternal uncle's daughter. They admit outsiders into their caste, but only immediately after birth and before the naval cord is cut off. They are government servants, lawyers, engineers, doctors, bankers,-priests, writers, land owners and husband men.

The Chitpavan Brahmans of the Deccan have no caste panchayats and no such system of organised interferences in domestic matters as that commonly found among lower castes. Their chief authorities are still their spiritual guides. In every town there is a Dharmadhikaris of the Sankaracharya of Sankeshwar who is the religious head of the community. Open breaches of caste rules and gross violation of *shastric precepts* are commonly dealt with by the agent in the public meetings of laymen and decision is passed by the majority of the votes. The penalties imposed are fines and religious penance or pain of excommunication. The fines are distributed among the priests of the town, though the Sankaracharya may claim a portion if he chooses. An appeal lies from the decision of the meeting to the Sankaracharya whose decision is final. The authority of the Sankaracharya is declining, and in sacred places such as Pandharpur, Kolhapur etc.; he is little more than a name. All castes disputes is these places are decided by the local priests without any reference to the Sankaracharya and they appropriately fine to themselves.

The Chitpavan Brahman of Goa are migrant from Maharashtra. They are pure vegetarian. In Goa, Chitpavans do not have any sub groups or sub-castes. They are divided into several exogamous gotras and their surnames are derived from these gotras names such as, Gadgil from the Gargi gotra, Apte from Atri, Marathe from Kapil, Vaze from Kashyap gotra etc.; Monogamy is the rule. Polygyny and polyandry are strictly prohibited among them. They perform an engagement ceremony prior to the marriage known as Sakharpuda. The actual marriage with a lengthy procedure consists of numerous stages. Simant pooja is one of them. The person who are attending the marriage, throw "akshata" on the couple and thus bless them. Kanyadan is done by the bride's father. The marriage symbol of the Chitpavans woman is Mangalsutra and green bangles. Residence after marriage is patrilocal. Dowry system exists but is not rigid. Divorce is allowed and a divorcee can remarry. They observed the puberty ritual on menarche.

The ceremony is restricted to the woman-folk. Chitpavans observe 11 days of pollutions after delivery. First cereal feeding or *Ushatavan* ceremony is observed for child when he attains the age of 6 months. Then after Jaiwal Ceremony (cutting of hair) and later on *Janaue* ceremony when the child is of 8-10 years. This time head shaving (mundane) is a must. The dead body is cremated with all Brahminical rituals. Several dieties are worshipped—the important ones being the Gramdevta or the village dieties like Shantadurga, Vijayadurga, Khalnath etc.; Mostly they are engaged in priesthood and cultivation.

Number of Females per 1000 males for this caste is given below (1931 census) :

Caste	District for which examined	Females per 1000 males
Chitpavan Brahman or Konkansasth	Poona, Satara, Kolaba, Ratnagiri	951

Proportion of literacy of females to 100 males

Caste	1993	1921	1911
Chitpavan Brahman	42	30	14

Variation in caste since 1881 (person'000).

Caste	1911	1901	1891	1881	
Chitpavan Brahman	111	114	117	—	
Variation	– 3	– 3	—	—	Total variation 1881-1911

(3) Anavalas/Anavil

Gujarati Brahman consists of ninety three subdivisions and Anavala is one of them who are all laymen or *grahastha*. Also known as Mastans and Bhathelas numbering 30,325 (males 10,036, females 14,289) at the Census of 1901 are found in the Surat district and the neighbouring Baroda territory. At present their concentration in the area is stretching from the river Tapi to the town of Vapi which covers surat and valsad districts. They are the best cultivators of South Gujarat. The name Anavala is derived from Anaval, a Gaikwar village and famous for it hot spring. The origin of the names Mastan and Bhathela is uncertain. Mastans according to one account, means proud or overbearing, a meaning which agrees well with the character of the former revenue farmers and village managers of this class. According to another account, Mastan is a shortened form of Mahasthan or great place, a name supposed to be the record of some former settlements of the tribe. It probably means the chief community of the South Gujarat and such phrases as Soni Mastan the Goldsmith community and Khadayata Mastan the Vani community, are in common local use. Of the term Bhathela, two explanations are offered; one would connect it with the caste of Bhats, the other would from bhat rice, means rice-man, a name well deserved by the Anavalas, the most successful rice-growers of South Gujarat. According to local tradition, Rama on his return from the conquest of Ceylon halted at a place called Patarvada in the hills of Bansda, about fortyfive miles South-East of Surat. Determined to hold a sacrifice, he required the services of a large body of priests. He searched the country round, and failing to find priests enough collected eighteen thousand of the hill-tribes and made them Brahmans. The legend that certain classes were made Brahmans by Rama, Krishna and other heroes and demigods is found in all parts of India. Unable to deny their claim to be Brahmans, the newcomers to the land, by the device of some local legends, want to show that the original settlers were Brahmans of a lower order than themselves. In the present case it seems probable that the founders of the class were Brahman who gathered round some early settler who had chosen the Anavala hot springs as the place of his hermitage. So, they are also known as *grahasths*.

They are pure vegetarian with jowar and rice being the staple food. They consume variety of pulses and grams, locally available fruits and vegetables. Tea and milk are common beverages. Some men smoke bidi and cigarette.

Almost all Anavala Brahmans worship Shiva. But as a class they are lax in religious observances and caseless in enforcing caste rules. Though obstinate and somewhat rough and quarrelsome, they are contented and orderly community, enterprising, friends to education, hospitable and liberal. Fifty years ago, almost all were peasants, and maintained Halis and though tillage is still the occupation of most, a considerable number is learning to read and write. Some have become village accountants, school teachers, lawyers and other traders in articles of food, and some entering government services. Socially, Anavala Brahmans are divided into an Upper or Desai class, the original colonists of South Surat and a lower or Bhathela class, the ordinary cultivators. During British rule, Desai enjoyed considerable power and wealth, claiming the rank of superior landlords, with the titles of Zamindar and Talukdars and possession of households of as many as four hundred dependants. The gradual extinction of the practice of farming resulting in the low land revenue (1803-1813 AD), and the establish-ment of the mass cultivators as direct holders from government, took away from the Desai, the source of much of their wealth. Many of them are said to have sunk into poverty, and falling into the hands of money-lenders, and thus have been forced to mortgage their lands and houses.

They eat with all members of their caste. Successful men among the lower class of Desai and the richer Bhathelas, anxious to improve their social position, try hard to marry their daughters into rich

---

Halis—Farm slaves are maintained not only by the Anavala Brahmans but by other castes in Gujarat.

Desai families. This rivalry for the hands of men of good family has led to some unusual practices. Polygamy is not uncommon. A Desai who finds himself in diffi-culties marries another wife, receiving from the brides father money enough to enable him to pay off his debts. Another result of the rivalry is that expenses consequent upon marriage such as payments in honour of the bride being sent to her husband's house, in honour of pregnancy, of the birth of a child, and on other occasion, are made not by the husband but by the wife's father. So heavy are these charges and such large sums are required as marriage portions, that among the Desai's, some families in which daughters have been numerous, have fallen into debt and been forced to mortgage their lands and houses. Cases have occured in which, for this reason girls have remained at their father's house till they have reached the age of eighteen or twenty. Under these circumstances the birth of a girl in a Desai's family is looked on as a calamity.

Opposite to this the fortune of Bhathela peasants have improved during the British rule. In the Surat villages the largest holdings, the richest crops, the finest cattle and the best built houses belongs to Bhathelas. It was reported that during ten years (1886-1896 AD) important changes had taken place in respect of marriage customs also, such as reduction in marriage expenses, to stop polygamy and to marry their girls among themselves without reference to Kul or family. The movement was so successful that most of the Desai's did not at that time get large sums of money on account of their son's marriages.

Among the Anavalas, these are twelve exogamous gotras of equal status, Basistha, Apri, Osnas, Batsab, Parasar, Gautam, Galab, Angastha, Kashyap, Kanab, Garg and Sankhayan. They have equal status. The

Anavalas are very much aware of the *varna* system and place themselves in the category of Brahman varna though other Brahmans considers them socially inferior. The marriage symbol for a woman is a red mark (Chandla) on the forehead at the hair parting. Eldest son succeeds as the head of the family. Lap-filling (Khola-bharani) is the pre-birth ritual among the Anavalas. Chhati is performed on the sixth day after a birth and followed by the tonsure, and Janaeu ceremonies. The important rituals connected with marriage are betrothal (Mangani), Pithi, Kanyadan, the tying of Mangalsutra and circumambulation of the sacred fire (*phera*). Dowry is given both in cash and kind and is known as Vankhdo. The rules of residence is patrilocal. There is no ban on either party from seeking divorce. In such event children are given to the custody of the father. Remarriage is not allowed for woman and in recent times there has been an upward trend in the marriageable age.

The family pattern includes both the nuclear as well as the extended type. Avoidance relationships are maintained between daughter-in-laws and father-in-laws. Similarly joking relations also exist between sister-in-laws and brother-in-laws and between grand parents and grand children. Male equigeniture is the rule of inheritance.

Anavil woman occupy a low status compared to that of their men-folk. They participate in social, ritual, economic and religious activities alongwith men but a woman does not enjoy powers of decision making. Neither do they have right over ancestral property nor have a role in the mechanism of social control or political sphere. They mainly look after family expenditure and households management. The dead are cremated and they observe death pollution for twelve days and perform the *shradh*, *masik*, *trimasik chhomasik* and *varsi* rituals, alongwith ancestral worship.

They are followers of both the Vaishnavite and Shaivite sects of Hinduism. Their family diety is Suklaswar Mahadev though they also worship Kalkamata, Krishna Bhagavan, Hanumanji, Ram and Sitlamata etc. They visit Hindu religious shrines of Puri, Benaras, Kedarnath, Badrinath. Holi, Deepawali, Janmastami are the major festivals. They avail of the services of Audhich Brahmans and Modh Brahmans in the performance of life-cycle rituals. They have faith in witchcraft and other male-volent forces. Some of their rituals are connected with agriculture. Cow is sacred to them and in the month of *Bhado* (August-September) their women worship the cow and observe fast.

They accept both cooked and uncooked food from other Brahman groups of the region. They also accept uncooked food from the Banias, Suthar, Kunbis but never accept any kind of food from the Vankars, Bhangis and Chamars. For economic reasons, they maintain close relations with the Dublas, Koli, Naika, Kokana and Dhodia who constitute the main force of agricultural labour. They share the facilities of well and other water resources, roads, schools, panchayat office with other castes. Cultivator-labourer relationship exist in the society.

The Anavala Brahmans of the Surat district settle their social disputes at meetings of the village castemen under the chairmanship of one of their member whom they select. Every head of a family is a member of the village panchayat. The penalties imposed on offenders are fines and *prayaschitta* (*penance*) or pain of excommunication. The fines are generally spent on caste dinners, purchase of vessels

The following table illustrates the origin of the Muhial/Mohyals sections and sub-sections:-

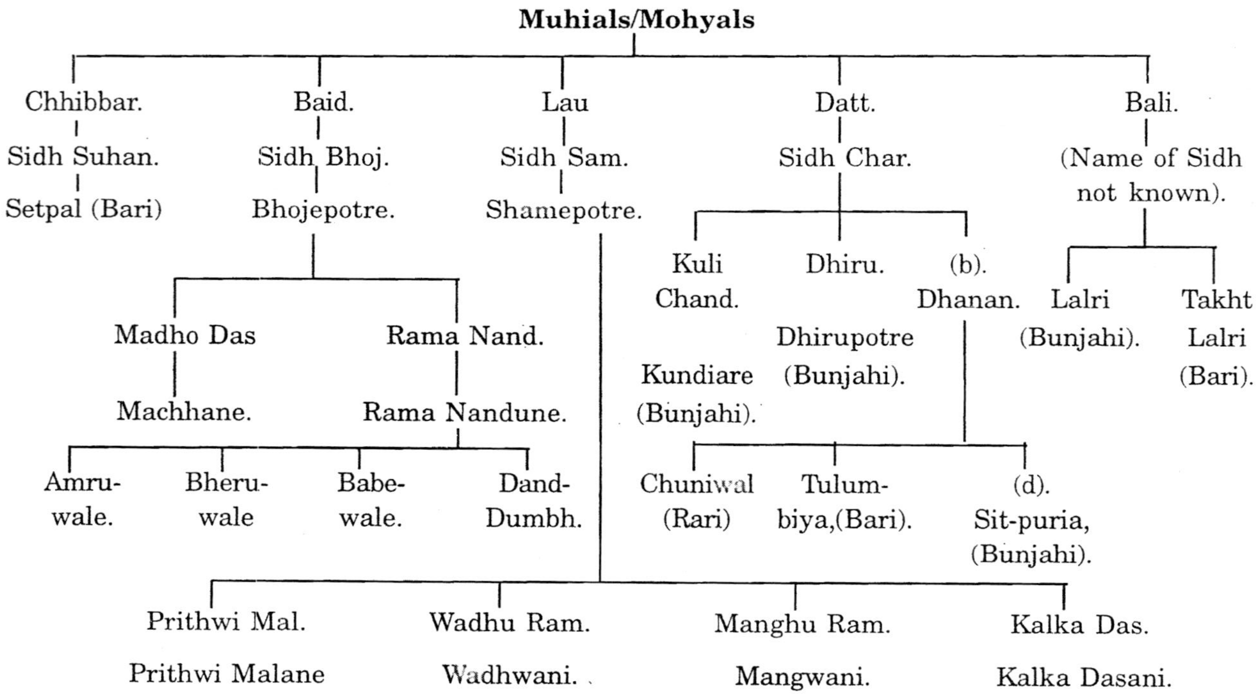

for the use of the caste and the like. In some places they are utilised for educational Purposes.

(4) Mohyal/Muhial Brahman

The origin of the Muhials has been described in following way. In Sambat 200 Vikrami the five Sidhs went to the Naunuthi Hill and there practised asceticism. About that time too the Khatris of the Arora family (now the Aroras) and the other Khatris fell out, so the latter separated from the Aroras and became *jajmans* of the Sihs. The Muhials who did not attach themselves to the Aroras refused to accept alms (*dan*) and are still purely secular. They are found chiefly if not exclusively in Rawalpindi (where many are Sikhs); in Jhelum and Shahpur as landholders or in service. All Muhials may marry girls of Brahman families which are not Muhial. It is named after seven Muhins or clans of which they consists. Another story derives their name from Mava, now a deserted place.

This caste community also hails from Jammu and Kashmir, but they originally inhabited most parts of Pakistan. However, after the partition they migrated and are now spread in some parts of India, as in Punjab and Jammu and Kashmir. In Jammu and Kashmir, they reside in Rajouri, Jammu, Poonch, Udhampur, Badherwah, Kishtwar, Akhnoor and in the Kashmir valley. Some of them are also known as Husaini Brahman, as one of them offered his sons to fight on the side of Hussain in the battle of Karbala. Some of them also prefix *Bhai* to their names. It is said that Mati Dass Chhiber was slain by the Mughal Emperor Auranzeb for refusing to Convert to Islam. Guru Teg Bahadur conferred on him the title of Bhai Mati Dass Chibber. The Muhials are progressive community. Their class, gotra and its origin are given below:-

Clan	Gotra	Origin
1. Datt	Bhardwaj	Descended from Drona Acharya, military tutor to the Pandavas and son of Bhardwaj. From his other son Dhanwantar vaid, descended.
2. Vaid	"	"
3. Chhibar	Bhargav	Descended from Parasuram
4. Bali	Parasher	Descended from Parashar through Balmik.
5. Mohan	Kashyap	——
6. Lau	Bashisth	——
7. Bhimwal	Koshal	Descended from Koshal Desh

It is also suggested that the name Muhial is derived from Mahi, 'land', so that it means 'land holders', and a connection is claimed with the Bhumihar community of Bihar and U.P. They like the Chibbars, claims descent from Parasuram.

The origin assigned to the class-names are curious. Datt is seen as the corruption of 'Aditya', 'law giver', and some hold that it means given or bestowed in adoption'.

The Chibbars claims that their ancestor Narsingh Deo lived at Mathura and moved through Bhatinda to Bhatner.

The Vaids appear to claim descent from Rai Gorakh Rai, a courtier of Rai Pithora.

The lau clan is closely associated with Bajwara, the old capital of Hoshiarpur district. Ballar Sain, son of Inder Sain Lau has aided Timur in his mission and thus Timur has granted him the fief of Bajwara.

The Bhimwals claim descent from the Raja Nandana, who held the fort of that name in Jhelum tehsil.

The Mohans also found favour with Timur, who appointed one of them as his Dewan. They also claim to obtained a grant of Mamdot in Jagir from Ala-ud-din Khilji early in the 14th century.

Mathura was also the earliest home of the Balis and their ancestor Tarloknath accompanied the Princes Dharopat and Shripat when exiled from that territory, together with an ancestor of the Bhimwals.

They are mostly non-vegetarian but refrain from eating beef. Wheat and rice are their staple diet. They are known for their headgear (dastar), speed (raftar) and their way of talking (guffar). The Mohyal are essentially an endogamous group at the community level and marriage between blood-relation is prohibited. The marriage age is mostly above twenty years for either sex. Monogamy is the most common form of marriage. Payment of dowry is in vogue. Divorce and remarriage are permitted in the community. Nuclear families predominate over other types among them. The Mohyal follows the Hindu law of inheritance. Women participate in social ritual and religious activities. They observe pollution for birth and death for ten and thirteen days respectively. They observe first feeding of cereals, besides the naming ceremony in childhood. Janaeu ceremony marks the formal initiation of males into Brahmanistic fold. Marriage is solemnized at the bridegroom's residence; officiated by Brahman priest. The marriage ceremony consists of reception of barat, lagan, exchange of garland, and send off. In certain cases a Muhial may take a bride from an ordinary Brahman family and this has frequently been done by the noblest Muhials but the converse case would not be tolerated. The death are cremated and they also perform annual death rites for their ancestors. Female infanticide was once practised among the Muhials, especially by the Chhibars and Datt. Three excuses were advanced for it. firstly; the cost of dowries; secondly, the difficulty of protecting women in times of war and thirdly, the artificial restriction of the marriage circles due to inter-tribal rules.

The descendants of the five Sidhs as refered above are further sub-divided into *panchtolias* (who give their daughters not less than 5 *tolas* of gold as dowry) and *tritoliyas* (who give their daughters not less than 3 *tolas* of gold as dowry). The latter rank below the former.

The traditional occupation of Mohyal is agriculture. However, a large number of them are in defence services. Of late, they have diversified into various occupations like trade, commerce, industry and government or private services. They also observe Hindu festivals and visits temples. They donot traditionally accept cooked food from low-caste Hindus.

(5) Nambuthiri

Among the Dravadian Brahman are classed the Nambuthiris also known as Kerala or Malayala Brahmans. The word is derived from Nambuka (to trust) and thiri (Sacred). There is another derivation of the word from nam (knowledge) and purikka (to impart). As the pre-historic heirs to the entire land of Kerala, the Nambutiris live on agriculture. Of the two division, Nambutiri and Nambutiripad, the latter are supposed to be stricter, and rank higher than the former.

Iyer (1981) states that 'the appearance of the Nambuthiris are generally very handsome and their complexion is of various shades. Their average height is 162 centimetres. They are well nourished and rotund. The hair on the head is plentiful, glossy and wavy. The tuft of hair or the *kudumi* is tied into a knot hanging over the forehead or at one side according to the fancy of the wearer and sometimes it is so done as to spread over the head. Gingelly oil is used to keep the hair smooth and make it grow long. This custom of having an oval patch, it is said, originated from an ordinance of Parasurama who had the tuft of the first colonists changed to the front for a national purpose. After bath, they wear on their forehead the horizontal saivite mark *tripundram* with *bhasmam* or *ashes*, and the vertical vaishnavite mark with *gopichandanam*.

'The Nambuthiri women are generally very fair. Being strictly *gosha* (seclusion to avoid being seen by men and women of other communities), the women shut themselves up inside their houses and seldom move about except on extreme urgency. They then shelter themselves behind broad round cadjan umbrellas specially made for the purpose, which are turned against the passersby and from behind whose cover they cast their sparkling eyes beyond to have a look at the passing stranger. They have long and glossy hair which is parted at the crown and drawn tight to the ears with a knot at the back. After a bath, they put horizontal lines on their foreheads with sandal paste'.

With regard to the dress pattern of the Nambuthiri as described by Iyer (1981), changes have been noted with the exception to that of a temple priest who still wears a piece of cloth reaching upto the knee and a small cloth (*thorthumundu*), over the shoulders and the chest. Others wear dhoti (*veshti*) which covers upto the feet and wear shirts and banians also. Earlier, *antharjaanam*, i.e. Nambuthiri women, who were in *gosha* were not wearing blouse (*ravikka*) and sari, are now wearing *set mundu* and blouse. Some of them have started wearing regular sari and blouse.

The Nambuthiri are strict vegetarian and traditionally do not take garlic and onion. Rice is the staple food. They use pulses like *gram*, *tur*, *urad*, *moong*, *peas* and *beans*. Cooking medium is Gingelly oil and coconut oil. They consume roots, tubers and vegetables. Only nonalcoholic drinks like tea, coffee and tender coconut are consumed. Milk and milk products like curds, butter, buttermilk and ghee are used abundantly. Betel-chewing with tobacco, betelnut and lime paste is common among both the sexes. Men use snuff. Earlier, they were not using onion, garlic, tomato etc., considering them as *nishedam* (to be avoided). These days younger generations have started consuming them. On *Amavasya*, *Pournami*, *Ekadasi* and *Dwadasi* and on other occasions, they do not eat brinjal, onion, tomato etc. Women during confinement and after delivery are not given roots and tubers.

Traditionally the Nambuthiri were confidential advisors and trusted friends of the rajas and chiefs. Thurston has compiled five sub-divisions of the Nambuthiri :-

(a) **Thampurakkals** : This term is a corruption of the sanskrit name 'Samrat' or Soverign which seems to have some reference to temporal and secular authority. They are entitled to (1) Bhadrasanam, (ii) Brahmasamrajyam, (iii) Brahmavarchas, (iv) Sarvamanyam.

(b) **Adhyans** : They form eight families and belong to different gotras. They donot perform yagams. Their women are distinguished from other women by their mode of dressing, their caste marks, etc. They are privileged to wear silver bangles, while others can wear only pewter or bell-metal bangles.

(c) **Visishta Nambuthiris** : These are of two classes, i.e., Agnihothris and Bhattachiris and of the former there are three divisions, i.e., Akkithiris, Somathiris and the Bhattathiris.

(d) **Samanyas** : They are ordinary Nambuthiris who study the Vedas, perform religious services in the temples and practice magic.

(e) **Jatimatras or Jatimatranmar** : The eight leading physician families of Malabar, or Ashta Vaidyas, are, by an inexcusable misuse of language, called Gatimatras or nominal Nambutiris. The class of Nambutiris called Yatrakalikkar (a corruption of Sastrakalikkar) also comes under this head. They are believed to be the Brahmans, who accepted the profession of arms from their great founder. Those that actually received the territory from the hands of Parasuram, called Gramani Nambutiris or Gramani Adhyas, are also Gatimatras. They were the virtual sovereigns of their respective lands. The physicians, the soldiers, and the landed kings, having other duties to perform, were not able to devote all their time to Vedic recitations. The mutalmura or first study was, of course, gone through. In course of time, this fact was unfortunately taken by the religious conscience of the people to lower the Brahmans who were deputed under the scheme of Parasuram for special functions in the service of the nation in the scale of Nambutiri society, and to mean a formal prohibition as of men unworthy to be engaged in Vedic study.

(f) **Sapagrasthas** : They are the receiver of the curse who have questioned the divine nature of Parasuram. The Nambuthiri are distributed in Trichur, Cochin, Trivandrum, and Palghat districts of Kerala. They speak Malayalam and Tamil, at home and use the Malayalam script.

They are below medium statured, have a broad head with a medium nose and a long face (Guha, 1935). They are pure vegetarian. Rice and curry is their staple cereal.

(g) **Payyannur Gramakar** : The Nambuthri are further divided into *othullavar* (vedic) and *othillathavar* (nonvedic). The former are privileged to recite and expound the Vedas, and perform the 16 ceremonies (*shodasa kriyas*), while the latter can neither study the Vedas nor superintend the performance of the above ceremonies. The Jatimatras and Sapagrasthas belong to the latter class. In all respects the observances of the two classes are similar. But these divisions are disappearing now. Earlier, their Smrithi prohibited them from studying English, as it is the language of Mleschas or the unclean. But, now, all of them are highly qualified, holding high positions in society. The community's self-perception and perception of it by other communities is high.

The Nambuthiri now marry within their own caste. They have different exogamous *gotras* like Srivatsa, Vishwamitra, Vasishta, Bharadwaja and Kashyapa. The Payyannur group married within the 16 families of the village. The Nambuthiri girls were married before reaching puberty in the past. But these days, only adult marriages are practised and age at marriage for girl is from 20 to 23 years and for boys from 25 to 30 years. Mode of acquiring mate is by negotiation. Monogamy is the form of marriage. Polygamy (nonsororal) is also allowed. The *thali* is the marriage symbol. Dowry in cash and kind exists. Rule of residence after marriage is patrilocal. Earlier, divorce was not permissible, whereas now, divorce is permitted to both the sexes with social approval. Remarriage is permitted for divorcee.

Both nuclear and vertically extended families exist among the Nambuthiri. Avoidance is observed between mother-in-law and son-in-law and between daughter-in-law and father-in-law, Joking relationship is permitted between brothers-in-law and grand-parents with grandchildren. Points of conflict and confrontation is property. The property of the Nambuthiri is called 'Brahmaswam'. Earlier, it was the eldest son who could inherit and maintain it. But nowadays, property is shared equally among all children. Father is the head of the family (*karnavan*) who is succeeded by the eldest son, while among the Payyannur branch the office of the *karnavan* was succeeded by the nephew. Nuclear families are on the increase. Equigeniture has become a common practice among the Nambuthiri.

The status of the Nambuthiri women, is slightly better now when compared to the status they enjoyed in the past. Earlier, they were kept in *gosha*. But, at present, they have discontinued this practice and take an active role in the economic, social and religious activities. In the past, women were not educated as it was against the norms; now they are well educated, employed and also able to make own decisions.

Pre-delivery rituals like *pumsavanam* and *seemantham* or parting of the hair is performed by the Nambuthiri in the fourth, sixth or eighth month of pregnancy. These are performed at a woman's first pregnancy, with a view to purify her and protect her from evil influences. Certain medicinal substances are given on this day. To make her cheerful and happy, musical performances are arranged.

After delivery, ten days of pollution is observed. In the past, barber women used to act as midwife. The touch of a *sudra* woman and taking meals in her presence entails no pollution during the period of confinement. Nowadays, they go to hospitals for delivery. On the 11th day, the mother and the child bathe and become purified after a purificatory ceremony of *punyaham*. The sanctified water is sprinkled on her and the child and around the whole house to remove pollution. She wears newly washed clothes which is supplied by the washerwoman. Only after forty days, she is allowed to take part in all the ceremonies, but can approach her husband only after ninety days.

Namakaranam or naming ceremony is conducted on the 12th day after the birth of a child. *Anaprasanam* or first rice giving is performed when the child is six months old. *Chowlam* or *tonsure* is performed for all the children when they are of three or five years of age. In case of boys, *kudumi* or tuft is kept after a shave. *Karnavedam* or boring is done on the day of *chowlam*. *Vidyarambam* is conducted at the age of five on the day of Vijayadasami or *pujaeduppu* day, i.e., the tenth day of the Dasehara. The father or guardian initiates him or her into the knowledge of letters. *Upanayanam* is performed when the boy is seven or eight years old.

Vayasariyunnada or puberty rite for a Nambuthiri girl is performed after observing three days of pollution. On the fourth day of puberty, accompanied by four Nayar women, the girl bathes and puts on washed clothes. On the fifth day, *punyaham* or purification is done.

Earlier, child marriages were common. Now-a-days, marriages take place only after puberty. The father or the brother of a girl chooses the bridegroom for her, after consulting the astrologer and if the horoscopes of both the girl and the boy agree, then they negotiate on dowry to be given to the bridegroom. On an auspicious day, marriage takes place in the bride's place. After performance of ritual formalities, the bride is taken to the bridegroom's house and *dikshaverikkuka* is performed for three days. On the fourth day, the consummation of marriage takes place in the bridegroom's house. Patrilocal form of residence is followed by them.

In the past, the eldest son of the Nambuthiri alone could marry in their own community, while the younger members would console themselves by forming fugitive alliance with women outside their own community. The Nambiyar, Nayar, Variyar and Tamburan were the communities who were involved in *sambandham* to the Nambuthiri. The eldest son could marry two or three women from the Nambuthiri community. But, the trend has changed with the work of 'Nambuthiri Yogakshema Sabha'. Now, all brothers can marry from the same community.

The Nambuthiri cremate their dead. When a person is at the point of death, *cheviyil othal* or *karana mantram* takes place, i.e. verses of Rigveda are whispered into his/her ears. The legs of the body are straightened and it is placed on three pieces of the bark of a plantain tree. The bier is made ready by the *cheetiyars*, i.e. Maran. The pyre which is made with the branches of a mango tree is consecrated by the recital of *mantrams*. The dead body is placed, head facing to the south. The pyre is lit with the sacred fire already prepared. *Udakakriya* or libation of water and offering of rice balls are made on all the ten days. *Sanchayanam* or the collection of the bones is done on the fourth day, and the same is buried underneath a tree or immersed in flowing water. On the 11th day, the chief mourner performs *sradha* or *ekodhistam*; the wife and sons of the deceased offer *pindams* individually. They all return home after a bath and take a dose of *punyaham*. The chief mourner undergoes *diksha* for one year and performs *nitya sradham*.

At the end of the year, *sapindakarana sradha* is performed. If a baby died it was buried. Ancestor worship is observed. In the past, if a woman dies before marriage, before her cremation, a nearest relative ties *thali* to the body and then funeral obsequies are performed. But now, all these formalities are curtailed and are vanishing.

Land is the Nambuthiri's main natural resource. Many of them are landlords. Lands are owned by individual proprietors. Their traditional occupation is settled cultivation and priesthood. The Nambuthiri can be categorised into different occupational groups, some are learned professionals and have the privilege of making sacrifices; some practice medicine, sorcery, magic, astrology and astronomy; some perform pujas in temples. Many are lecturers, doctors, engineers, businessmen etc. Earlier, they were letting out their lands to the Nayar tenants, for cultivation. But, nowadays, they employ labourers to cultivate the land. Wages are paid in both cash and kind. Iyer (1981) wrote, 'once upon a time the Nambuthiris were the minister of the Rajas, their judges, their generals in the field, and above all, their spiritual preceptors'. Now they are employed in both government and private services and some own factories, run clinics and some others are hereditary priests.

The 'Nambuthiri Yogakshema Sabha' exists for the upliftment of the community. This Sabha has brought in impressive reforms among them in the removal of *aitham* pollution and *gosha*, in educating the women and in the removal of *kudumi* or tuft and changing them to modern hair styles. The Sabha also played an important role in changing the marriage rules that was adopted earlier, i.e., the eldest son marrying three or four Nambuthiri women and younger brothers having relationship outside was stopped and all sons can now marry within the same community as mentioned earlier. Monogamy is the rule of marriage now.

The Nambuthiri are worshippers of Vishnu, Siva, Bhagawati and Ganapati. They are nonsectarian in religion. *Saligrama* puja is generally performed by all the Nambuthiris. Homage is paid to Brahma, Vishnu and Siva, through images or worship of five stones which are believed to be permeated by the essence of the five chief dieties. The five stones are: 1. the black stone representing Vishnu, 2. the white stone representing Siva's essence, 3. the red stone representing Ganesha, 4. the small piece of a metallic stone representing the wife of siva and 5. the piece of crystal representing the Sun. They perform puja both at home and at temple. They visit all sacred centres, and celebrate Hindu festivals like Onam, Vishu, Thiruvadirai and Krishna Janmashtami. The 'Yogakshema Sabha' which had actively campaigned for social reforms is not very active now. Sacred specialists from the same community perform all rituals, worship and give religious teaching.

Some members of the Nambuthiri, both male and female, have been trained in playing stringed instruments and classical music and have passed examinations. Some of them have expertise in classical dance.

In nut-shell, the selection of persons for marriage is guided mainly by two rules: firstly, they are not be outside the family and secondly, they must be inside the caste. Monogamy is the form of marriage and polygyny (non-sororal) is allowed. A kind of mixed marriages sometimes takes place among them in some parts of the state. Nambuthiri girls are married both before and after they reach the age of puberty. From the date on which the settlement is made, the girl is regarded as betrothed and after that different ceremonies takes place in various phases. Social division exists at the gotra level. Its function is to regulate marriage alliances and indicate one's descent. A marriage pendant (*thali*) is the symbol of married women. The Nambuthiri follow partilocal residence. Widow remarriage is prohibited. Nuclear families are more common than the vertical extended ones. Earlier, inheritance was made equigeniture but now succession passes on to the eldest son. Pre-birth rituals include Pumsavanam and Seemantham, The delivery of a Numbuthiri woman takes place on the bare floor. The umbilical chord is cut by a barber woman who is a midwife. Birth pollution lasts for ten days. They observe Punyaham, naming (Namakaranam), first rice-giving (Annaprasanam), tonsure, earboring and Upanayanam. The marriage rituals involved are Nandimukh, Punyaham, Panigrahanam, Saptapati, and Dikshanerikkukal. The dead are cremated and rituals observed are Sanchayanam, Shradha, Punnyaham and Nitya Shradham. Only married men are qualified to perform the sacrifices. Liquor and flesh are strictly forbidden to the Nambutiris. They are not permitted to swear, or take oath in any way. A Nambutiris observe 64 anacharams, or irregular customs, which are said to have been promulgated by the great reformer Sankaracharya. Some of the festivals observed by the Numbutiris are : Sivaratri, Upkarnma, Nagarapanchimi, Gokulashtami, Navaratri, Chaturthi, Puram, Onam, Vishu etc.; The Kathakali (Dance) is held in great esteem and favour by the Nambutiris. Among plants the *tulsi* or sacred basil is the most sacred of all.

The traditional occupation of the Nambuthiri are settled cultivation and priesthood. They are also engaged in business and government or private services. A caste council the Nambuthiri Yogakshema Sabha, has been formed for the welfare of the community. They are Hindu, and their sacred specialists are from the same community. Traditionally, the Nambuthiri accept from and exchange food with the Brahman only. They accept water and Sidha food from other communities like the Nayar and Kshetriya. Formal education for boys and girls is favoured and they study upto post graduate level. They make use of the modern medicare system, and modern methods of family planning. In addition, they utilise other welfare programmes initiated by the government.

References

- Mr. D.R. Bhandarkar draw attention to the striking similarity between certain Chitpavan names and the name of places in Palestine.
- Bombay Gazetteer, volume IX, part-I, pp. 4-6.
- Ibbetson, Denzil, "Punjab Castes", 1993, Low Price Publication, Delhi.
- Iyer, A. Krishna, L.K., 'The Tribes and Castes of Cochin, Vol-III, 1981, Cosmo Publications, New Delhi.
- Crooke, W., 'The Tribes and Castes of the North-Western India, 1974, Vol-I, Cosmo Publication, New Delhi.
- Enthoven, R.E., 'The Tribes and Castes of Bombay, Vol.I, 1920, Cosmo Publications, New Delhi.
- Risley H.H., 'The Tribes and Castes of Bengal Vol. I & II, Calcutta Firma Mukhopadhyay.
- Singh, K.S., People of India, Vol. XXII, 2003 Gujarat, Popular Prakashan Pvt. Ltd., Mumbai.
- Singh, K.S., People of India, Haryana. Vol. XXIII.
- Singh, K.S; People of India, Kerala.
- Thurston, Edgar and Rangachari, K., 'Castes and Tribes of Southern India', Vol. V, Asian Educational Services, New Delhi, 1993.

8

Caste : Change and Continuity

Change in any sphere is a universal law and what type of shape it will take depends on various factors. In case of Bhumihar caste, changes are taking place in its every sphere of life, be it, economy, polity, cultural or social.

The notion of ascribed status, hierarchy and ritual purity and pollution have been under attack time and again by the new knowledge and ideologies. A trend now visible seeks seperate organizations for each of the twice born varnas on social and political platforms. Thus there is a "Swami Sahajanand Saraswati Samiti or Brahmarshi Samaj" Organisation on social and political front. Another militant front is "Ranveer Sena" on socio-economic front, dealing with it. They do meet from time to time to listen to their important leaders and pass resolution on a variety of subjects, including the need for internal social reform and the desirability of political solidarity. Varna loyality has also been invoked to secure political support in elections. Among subjects on which they mostly passes resolutions are, simplification of rituals, avoidance of wasteful expenditure on rites and rituals and marriage ceremonies, political parties whom to vote etc; but in this context their say do not work very much due to democratization of views of different people of Bhumihar society and their preference to vote certain political leader/parties etc. But no doubt, because after independence, jati has been gradually politicalised (Ref. Kisan Sabha and Ranveer Sena: Its movement) and is believed to play an increasingly important role in elections. It has been exploited for political ends by various political parties. The realities of ground level politics compel them to keep the "caste equation" constantly in view. To meet the situation two strategems can be adopted: either two or more rivals political parties put up candidates belonging to the same jati or, to divide jati votes, they secretly encourage independents from the jati to contest against the candidates of the rival political party. This trend vitiates the atmosphere and gives rise to inter-jati tension and conflicts, as is seen in the areas of Jehanabad, Patna, Bhojpur districts etc; And in this process the victimized are from vulnerable sections and also from the dominant castes of the society.

This rise in caste tension has posed a major challenge to India's polity and will test its capacity for conflict-resolution and problem-solving. Political distortions have also created problems for this caste (Bhumihar).

There are at least three significants influences on the cultures-**westernization, emergent national cultural styles,** and **popular culture**. The last one is largely a product of the mass media. The impact of films, radio and TV has tremendous impact in reshaping one's images and attitudes. Their aesthetic quality may be (of) sub-standard, but their hold on the people is undeniable. Some of the styles and other cultural values conveyed by these media are widely emulated in various parts of the country by different sections (including Bhumihars) of the people. Folk arts and cultures of Bhumihars have also undergone sea-change due to the above.

Similarly several factors account for the erosion of the family and kinship in Bhumihar i.e.; modern education, new occupations, geographical mobility, impact of mass media and so forth. Now greater choice of marriage is available and in many places intercaste marriages are taking place among this caste. In recent years, Bhumihar families have begin to advertise in different leading newspapers in matrimonial columns and also through internet for their sons and daughters marriage. This may be due to hardship faced by the parents of marriagable children.

More educated women are preferring to work outside the home and in the metropolitan and big cities it has become necessities for them to supplement their husband's income. Due to this interdinning and interpersonal relations, Divorce, remarriages etc; are taking place in much bigger way. Elders are also feeling neglect and losing their respect.

Erosion has also taken place in Jajmani system due to spread of urban culture and monetary economy. Jati panchayats also appear to be on the decline and mostly younger generation are not taking it seriously. This has led to the rise in crime and other evils in this caste because now no fear is there for their misdeeds.

Changes in dress pattern and the style of living has also taken place and most of the younger generations are not aware about their caste culture, norms, values and social relationship. All these are disturbing phenomenon for the said caste.

These changing ethos raises a number of questions. Why is the younger generation losing respect for the elder's, How will the growing demand for women's equality affects family patterns, castiest approach and increasing role of caste association in the political sphere for their own benefit etc., All these problems disturb the society as whole and the caste in particular, but the questions are not new. The problem solving instruments in the society has to be geared up to clear the obstacles and setbacks which the caste is undergoing. Solution has to be found in economic field and social justice, and also processes of participatory decision-making has to be initiated. While some aspects of tradition will survive because of their vitality and usefulness, many of the scaly prejudices of the past will have to be eradicated and structures of expolitation and tyranny must be demolished. The process is painful and it will also take time, but betterment and social cause of the caste in question has to take decision, What is right and what is wrong for them in earnest way and also for its future generation. Case studies of two villages to substantiate different aspects of Bhumihar caste which include change and continuity, dealt above is given below:-

These studies were carried out in two different linguistic belts of Bihar, namely, Dhangarha a Bhojpuri speaking area and secondly, Ismailpur a Maghi speaking area; to assess the changes that has and is taking place in respect of Bhumihar caste. Selection of these villages have been done on the basis of their social, economic and educational development. These have been further divided into sub variables, but many other Variables have been left out, keeping in view the nature of the study. So, on the basis of these limited variables, we cannot generalise the changing scenario in general but it gives us an opportunity to examine the changes and continuity which is being faced by the said caste at a close range.

Sample selection for both the villages were done on the basis of socio-economic and educational backgrounds of the respondents and further divided into other variables, which are given below in the table :

Table

Sample Selection from Dhangarha and Ismailpur:

Category		No. of Samples Dhangarha	Ismailpur
Caste :	Bhumihar		
Sex :	Male	10	10
	Female	10	10
Age :	15-30 yrs	4	4
	31-45 yrs	6	6
	46-60 yrs	6	6
	61 & above	4	4
Education :	upto Matric	8	13
	Matric & Above	12	7
Occupation :	Service	6	3
	Housewife	3	3
	Business	2	2
	Agriculturist	9	12
Family Income : (in Rupees)			
	upto Rs. 10,000/- P.A.	6	11
	Rs. 10,001 & above P.A.	14	9
	Total	20	20

50.0 percent of males and females each were interviewed to ascertain their views on different aspects related to the caste. Similarly other variables were kept in proportion to bring in objectivity to the subject matter which has been dealt with in the previous chapters. Analysis of the facts has been done in the light of changes and continuity that is taking or has been taken place.

(i) Dhangarha

It falls under the erstwhile Saran district and is now a part of Chapra district of the state (Bihar). It's under Baniapur police station and connected with pitched road from Chapra, a distance of 27 kms from the village. The state capital Patna is 90 kms away from the village and NH-101 passes nearby (1 km away) it. One can approach to this village by Bus and other private vehicles throughout the year.

Dhangarha derives it names from the "Garha Devi", who is also the village Goddesses. The village is spread over in an area of one and half sq. kms. 90.0 percent of the houses in village are made up of bricks and other materials, whereas 10.0 percent houses are Kuccha. Roads and bylanes are made up of bricks. Almost all the houses have handpumps. Infrastructural facilities available in the village are; Post office, Schools, Panchayat Bhawan, Health Sub-centre, Public library, Anganwadi Kendra, Cooperative Society; Government Handpump etc.;

The total population of the village is around one lakh (approx. 1500 HHS). 90.0 percent of population residing in this village are Bhumihar and most of them belongs to Domrait and Shandilya gotra; other castes form 10.0 percent of the total population, i.e.; Turha, Koeri, Kurmi and Muslim. Every year a large number of people assemble during the fair held at the Mosque of Maqdoom Saheb to pay their obeisance.

Marriage within Kins group take place in almost all the cases except one or two. The marriage is performed in accordance with the Vedic rites and rituals. Mostly marriage by negotiation takes place between groom's and bride's parents, but there is a relative relaxation of caste rules in respect of urban settled educated youth and rural youth. Before marriage settlement, now they want to know about their future bride and they are given chances to know each others.

Previously Dhoti-Kurta was in vogue at the time of marriage but now relaxation has been given to wear suits, but in case of bride, she has to wear embrodried Sari bought for this occasion. To save money and time, now most of the parents prefer to conduct thread wearing ceremony on this occasion whereas previously it was done at the age of 8-12 years. Even today some parents maintain this tradition, but their numbers are few and declining with each passing years. Inter caste and love marriages are rare. Even today, marriage of girls take place comparatively at lower age than the boys, because women in this respect (deciding girls marriage) plays an important role. They are more concerned about girls age (mensural and other rules of pollution). The tradition of second marriage known as "*gauna*", is dying fast due to compulsion on several fronts, which was observed with strictness in the past. The dowry system is on the rise and it has become impossible for many girls parents to find suitable grooms. Marriage proccedures has also been curtailed, previously it takes almost a month and every day a seperate rituals was observed, such as when girl enters boy house, they were taken into 'Kohbar' room. Now the system of "Kohbar" (an art form, painted on the wall of the room) is dying and younger generations (most of them) are not aware about it.

Every Bhumihar village has its Kul Devi/Devta and Gram Devi/Devta. Similarly they worship their "Kul Devta", known as "Bandi Devta" (which is kept in a vessel). But most of the peoples specially younger generation is not aware about the name and when worship takes place. As old people of this village recalls that during the month of August (Sawan) every year Kul Devta is worshipped and it is shown to the female head of the family, who in turn show it to others and also perform *puja*.

In recent years marriages are also taking place outside the region, which was not so in the past, due to strong Kinship affinity, which is loosing its importance day by day.

Previously sari were worn by the females/girls and Dhoti-Kurta/Bandi by the males/boys. But now-a-days girls and boys and even men prefer to wear modern dressess.

Death ceremony is also observed for ten days and lastly 'Shradh Karma' is done by the family member of the death for salvation of the death soul (Atma). But now due to urbanisation and modernisation, some persons prefers 'Arya Samaj' method and in 3-4 days period perform all the death rituals.

Caste and Occupation in the context of the Indian rural social order are inter-related. Each caste is more or less expected to pursue its prescribed occupation and at present 60.0 percent of the population are engaged in agricultural pursuits and the average land-holding size is 5-6 acres per family, which is decreasing day by day. It is followed by services (30.0%), business (10.0%) etc. Previously business was considered as low in status in this caste but now growing unemployment and lack of opportunity in service sector has driven the youth of this caste to join business in more numbers. Most of the lands are irrigated. Potato, rice and paddy are their main crops and also their staple diet. Due to increase in income from other sources (than agriculture), most of them have become well off economically.

Table : Occupational bifurcation of persons fo Dhangarha are given below:

Occupation	No. of Person
a) Engineers	17
b) Doctor	20
c) Administration	15
d) Education	50

Rest came under agriculturists, unemployed, students and Housewife.

Increase in Education level of the younger generations, as almost 85.0 percent of girls and 80.0 percent of boys of this village are literate, (literacy rate: 55.0 percent) has encouraged migration from this village to the towns/cities, which at present is around 30.0 percent. Also, 15.0 percent of the students are pursuing their higher education at Patna and Delhi University. Impact of education on them can be seen in the form of adopt new way of life style, liberal in thinking, changes in food habit, changes in custom, culture, values, norms etc.

This village falls under the Baniapur assembly constituency and dominated by the Bhumihar caste (Approx. 50.0% voters). The following table shows the changing scenario in the field of politics related to this caste for the above assembly segment.

Table : Baniapur Assembly Constituency

Election Year	Name of wining Candidate	Caste
1952	Sh. Bishwanath Singh	Bhumihar
1957-67	(Candidate Not recalled)	Congress Party won

Contd...

—	Smt. Uma Pandey	Bhumihar
1967-1977	—	Other Castes
1977	Dr. Ramakant Pandey	Bhumihar
1999	Sh. Dhumal Singh	Bhumihar

Similarly Baniapur Constituency falls under Maharajganj Parliamentary segment and at present is (mostly) dominated by OBCs and Muslim Communities. During 1977-79, Sh. Ramdev Singh represented this seat on Janta Dal ticket. At present Sh. Prabhunath Singh (a Rajput) represent this seat in the Parliament, on JD(U) ticket.

In between and upto 1977, persons from other castes won state assembly election and the reasons attributed by the respondents are (i) In-fighting among Bhumihar caste candidates, as more and more people contest election from the same caste dividing the vote bank, and (ii) Voters have become self-centred and interest conscious. They vote for those candidates who can serve their personal interest in more better way. Thus caste solidarity is now loosing the ground.

For spreading education in this area, few castemen have made efforts and one of them is Sh. (Dr.) Ramakant Pandey, once an MLA from Baniapur, established "Lokmanya Degree College", in Hafizpur.

A prominent freedom fighter of this area was Saryug Ojha, who died in 1942 in Chapra jail. He was involved in burning of Baniapur Dak-bunglow and police station during Independence movement. His compatriot was Kapildeo Singh of Sisai village. Besides Bhumihars, other castes from the area were also involved in freedom struggle such as, Kedarnath Puri (from Gosai caste).

(ii) Ismailpur

This village most probably derived its name from

Muslim rulers. It falls under Khizar Sarai Police Station under Gaya district and is 19 kms. away from district headquarter on Patna-Gaya road. One can approach this village by Bus or other Vehicles. The nearest railway station is Gaya. This village is spread over an area of 3 sq. kms. and having a population of 3,000 (270 HHS). Out of 270 HHS; approx. 200 HHS are of Bhumihar caste, rest of them are from other castes, i.e.; Yadav, Mochi, Mushar, Nai, Brahman etc., Bhumihars of this village belongs to Kashyapa Gotra. Their age-wise population breakdown is as follows:-

Table

Age	No. of Person
under 25 years	800
Above 25 years	1200

Most of the modern facilities except electricity (available since 1959) are not available in this village. For this they have to approach to other villages, as for Post Office, they have to move one km. away from village. Similarly, middle and high school is situated at Khizarsarai (3 kms away), Bank at Chiroli (2 kms) etc.; A "Gram Sudhar Samiti" exist in this village for the last 10 years. It manages village pond and uses it for commercial purpose, Devisthan etc. A few handpump exist in the village but mostly they fetch drinking water from the well.

Marriage is mostly settled by negotiation between groom's and bride's parents but now-a-days consent of groom's are taken before marriage. Boys are married between 20-25 years of age while for girls marriage age is 18-22 years. Marriage rites/rituals are observed in accordance with vedic system but with a relaxation. In one case, widow remarriage has also taken place but with resistance from the villagers which indi-cates that still they are traditional in their outlook. Cases of out-casting family from *biradari* has also came to light, but this phenomenon has become rare now-a-days. Jajmani system still prevails in the village but it is loosing its role. Villagers worship their Kul Devi/ Devta known as "Hiraman Baba" (a huge pind symbolises it). Every important works/occasions begin with worship of Kul Devi/Devta. Besides this Grih Devi/Devta, known as "Chachi-Mama" (established in every home) is worshipped by the householders on different occasions. Observance of death 'Shradh Karma' is strictly followed by the family members, and no relaxation is permitted.

Except few, all are land owners and the average land holding size is 5.0 acres per family. Soil is very fertile and irrigation facility is available in the area. Villagers cultivate two crops, namely, paddy and wheat, in a year. Besides this other crops such as potato, cash crops etc, are also cultivated. Use of agricultural machine has taken place in big ways in this village. Besides agriculture, about 50.0 percent villagers have entered into milk business. They have set up a Milk Collection Centre in this village through which milk is distributed. So, the migration rate is very low. Some persons are also employed in service sector (approx. 160 persons).

As there is no school in the village, students have to move to other places for their study and for higher education, they move to Gaya and Patna university. Despite this the literacy rate of the villagers are 55.0 percent. Boys are more educated than girls which also shows the traditional social attitude of the parents. Birth of son is associated with parents salvation (Moksha).

This village falls under Belaganj State Assembly segment. The following table indicate the relationship between caste and politics.

Table

Year	Name of winning Candidate	Caste
1952	—	—
1962	Sh. K.N. Singh (Congress)	Bhumihar (Son of Tekari Maharaja)
1967	Sh. M.P. Singh (Congress)	Bhumihar
1972	Sh. Jitendra Singh	Bhumihar
1977	Sh. Abhiram Sharma (Congress)	Bhumihar
1980-till date	—	Other Castes

Upto 1980's it was a strong hold of Congress and Bhumihar caste but after that, Yadavs took hold of it, which continue till date and now they win election from this assembly segment.

Similarly for Parliament election it falls under Gaya constituency. In 1967. Sh. Surya Prakash Narayan Puri (Budhauli Mahant) and by caste a Bhumihar won on Congress ticket. From 1971 to 1980, other castes won the Parliament seat. After 1980's, it became reserved Constituency and Sh. Ishwar Chaudhary of BJP won the election from this constituency. Sh. Ramji Manjhi (BJP) represent this seat in parliament (13th Lok Sabha). Later Sh. Rajesh Manjhi (RJD) hold this post.

One of the strongholds of Ranveer Sena this region is calm and peaceful. It is surprise to know that, there is no impact of this Sena on the villagers and they lead comparatively a peaceful life. However, sometimes, CPI foment agrarian unrest but by and large its impact on the villagers are negligable.

Comparative study of both the villages reveals following fact :- that (i) Both of them are traditional in respect of marriage system, custom, culture, values and norms but due to education they are changing in this direction.

(ii) Caste solidarity is becoming loose day-by-day due to outside factors which is influencing the said Caste in different ways.

(iii) Migration is less in Ismailpur village than Dhangarha due to education and outsiders contact, which is comparatively less in Ismailpur.

(iv) Jajmani system is fast decaying in Dhangarha than in Ismailpur village.

9

Conclusion

It has been customary to condemn caste as a critical institution which has been inhuman and unjust in its application and which has stagnated the Hindu religion, having outlived its utility. There have been writers who have pleaded for the retention of the system in a modified form, but there has been unanimity in the condemnation of the caste system as it is today. In view of this it is essential to draw attention to some important and significant socio-economic functions which the system has been fulfilling within the framework of Hindu society.

Looking at the system from the individual's point of view, it provides a security which no degree of unworthiness and incapability on his part will deprive him of unless, of course, he breaks the caste norms. He is assured of employment, shelter, protection and marriage. In the event of a disability he is not faced with disaster. In sum, caste is one's main line of defence in so far as it provides socio-economic security within a permanent milieu which is not based on changing individual caprices. Castes norms provide guidance to the individual in the ordering of his daily personal routine and social behaviour. By providing a common forum for collective effort and agitation, one's caste increases the chances of mobility for an individual. For example the Kayastha now regarded only next to the Brahman in North India were only a clean Sudra caste in the 18th century.

A caste provides free training and education to its members in the skills in which it is traditionally proficient.

One of the most important functions of the caste system has been to carve out a place for any kind of a group or community, whether it is social, occupational, racial or religious, within the broad framework of society without asking it to surrender its own individual way of life. Caste has made Hindu society a liberal federation. Integration is so varied in country as India could have been achieved only through such an ingenious system or through despotism and totalitarianism. It is the caste system which has provided a way for assimilating outside influences and groups, like the tribes for instance. Religious and social revolts which have been punished with death by burning and stoning by other higher religions, have resulted in India only in the addition of new castes to the main system. In fact, the caste system has provided an outlet for very strong individual capacities and a scheme for social adjustment which some writers have compared favourably with the european system of warring nationalities. Caste has bestowed uninterrupted internal peace on, and engendered stability within, the very heterogeneous Hindu society. Provided with such internal integration and strength, Hindu society has faced calmly and adequately disasters and catastrophes of immense magnitude, like external invasions, the proselytizing activities of Christians, coerced conversion to Islam, internal upheavals like the egalitarian movements dating back to Buddhism, and also natural crises like famines and earthquakes. It has put it stamp not only upon tribal social organization, but also on the daily life of Indian Christians and Muslims.

Basing itself on the *karma* theory, i.e., the belief that one's status in life is determined by one's actions in past incarnations, the caste system has provided not only justification for the present disabilities of the inferior castes, but what is socially more significant, also an excellent motive for the peaceful acceptance of the present conditions along with the incentive for efforts to perform what are socially regarded as good actions, in order to ensure a better future. By so providing for strict adherence to custom as also the possibility of a cure for frustration, social solidarity has been maintained uninterrupted by any conflicts.

Caste has also performed a silent function, though of only sentimental value. In Hindu society there is no peace of mind for a couple until they get a son, because without him there is no heaven nor peace hereafter. It has been found that inbreeding leads to a preponderance of males; and by prescribing endogamy the caste system has soothed the minds of thousands of generations of Hindus.

In view of the functions which the caste system has so excellently performed, scientific investigators like Hutton have pleaded that caste is a good institution which has proved its worth and should be reformed, not rooted out. Untouchability, exploitation of one caste by another and such other harmful concomitants of the system should be done away with, and not the whole system, the broken and poisoned finger should be amputated, not the whole hand.

The origination and continuation of sub-caste system (Bhumihar is one of them) has been fulfilling one's socio-economic and religious requirements till time immemorial and helped the society to strengthen bonds among themselves which in turn is essential for overall development of the human beings. No doubt the said caste is facing lots of problems these days, as for example, I have gone through many web sites on caste of Bihar and found news about Ranvir Sena and its massacres in rural areas. In the same web site, the "Asian Age", dated 24th June' 2000, one can find an article title 'Bihar's Bhumihar Stain', by Soroor Ahmed, in which this caste has not been put in the right perspective and has been blamed for most of thrills of the State. But this is not so and if one has to survive in the current situation of the state where 'survival of the fittest' rule is applicable, one has to protect one self and other castes in this respect is not lagging behind.

APPENDICES

Appendix A

According to 1996 estimates, Bhumihars in some of the Lok Sabha Constituencies in Bihar are given below:-

Name of Lok Sabha	Percent of Bhumihar among total Caste
Ballia	7.0
Begusarai	8.0
Arrah	5.0
Buxar	sizeable number
Gaya	6.0
Gopalganj	sizeable number
Jehanabad	9.0
Khagaria	5.0
Munger	5.0
Muzaffarpur	6.0
Nalanda	6.0

Nawada	7.0
Barh	6.0
Patna	7.0
Motihari	5.0
Bikramganj	sizeable number
Samastipur	5.0
Maharajganj	5.0
Vaishali	6.0

Source: Majid Hussain; "Encyclopaedia of India" (Bihar), Vol. XXVI, 1994, Rima Publishing House, New Delhi.

Appendix B

Some colleges in the name of Bhumihars/related to it.

G.D. College, Begusarai.
SKM College, Begusarai.
Dipnarayan Technical Training Institute, Barari.
B.P. Sinha Memorial College, Dhanbad.
Srikrishna Mahila College, Jehanabad.
SKR College, Barbigha, Munger.
LS College, Muzaffarpur.
Srikrishna Memorial College, Nawada.
J.J. College, Rambagh, Bihta.
Swami Sahajanand Sanskrit Mahavidyalaya, Bihta.
MD College, Naubatpur, Patna.
LP Shahi College, Patna.
Uma Pandey College, Pusa, Samastipur.
Sir Ganesh Dutt Memorial College, Patna.
Baijnath Pandey Arya Sanskrit College, Siwan.
Ram Dayalu Singh College, Muzaffarpur.
Mahesh Singh College, Muzaffarpur.

Appendix C

Castes/communities, segments, synonyms, surnames and titles are given below :-

(a) **Anavil/Anavala Brahman :**

Synonyms Bhattela, Mastan (Gujarat)

Titles : Desai, Mehta, Naik, Vashi (Gujarat)

Exogamous units/ clans : Balsa, Gulab, Kanab, Osria (Gujarat)

Gotras : Atri, Basistha, Batsa, Galava, Garg, Gautam, Kashyap, Parasar, Sankhayama, Vasisht (Gujarat)

(b) **Bhumihar/ Babhan :**

Synonyms : Bhumihar Brahmans (Bihar)

Grihasth Brahman, Zaminder Brahman (Uttar-Pradesh)

Groups/ Sub-Groups : Bawandia, Bijalpuri, Danenshiead, Dighayt, Dijalpuri Eksaria, Jat Jadia, Malitwar, Taliha, Taliyadia (Bihar),

Achariya, Athariya, Baghochhiya Bemuwar, Donwar, Jaithariya, Karerwa, Karmali, Kinwar, Kolhaniyan, Kolraha, Sakarwar (Uttar Pradesh)

Atharb (eponym) (H.H. Risley)

Sub divisions :- Athariya, Baghochhiya, Belhariya, Bemuwar, Bhaiwadh, Birramiya, Biruar, Chandasi, Domkatar, Donwar, Eksonya, Gantamiya, Jaithariya, Kachhi, Kahatwar, Kinwar, Kolaha, Kolaha, Kolhaniyan, Kolaha, Kolhaniyan, Kotraha, Karmali, Mirzapuri, Murao, Parasiya, Raikwar, Sabraniya, Sakarwar, Sam, Sorhaniya, Suroban, Titiha [W. Crooke]

Titles : Chaudhary, Pandey, Rai, Singh, Thakur, Tewari (Bihar), Akhwani, Arape, Chambe, Dikshit, Dube, Rai, Singh, Upadhaya (H.H. Risley)

Surnames : Mishra, Pandey, Pandit, Sharma, Tewari (Bihar)

Exogamous (gotras) units/clans : Bhardwaj, Gautam, Didhvait, Jaltaria, Kashyap, Sakarwar, Sandilya Vatsa (Uttar Pradesh)

Gotra : Bhardwaj, Sandilya (Bihar)

Angiras, Bhargena, Gargye, Gobhila, Kasyapa, Katyana, Parasara, Vasishth, Vatsya (W. Crooke)

Sections : Abkahon, Aggechal, Agnidhaut, Agmihotra, Ajaitia, Akasaria, Ambaria, Anarai, Anraya, Anwar, Araich, Arait, Arewar, Arnwait, Aswaria, Athrab, Athrol, Athrul, Anigh, Baid, Bachgotra, Badonia, Bagaudia, Bagri, Baksaria, Balaiar, Barnia, Budramia (H.H. Risley)

Exogamous unit/lineages (*vans*, *khandan*) : Bihar.

(c) Mohyal, Muhial Brahman

Groups/ Sub-Groups: Husaini Brahman (Jammu and Kashmir)

Titles : Bakshi, Bali, Bunwal, Chilbas, Dutt, Lali, Mohan, Vaid (J&K)

Gotra : Bhardwaj, Kasab, Parasram (J&K)

(d) Nambuthiri

Groups/sub-groups : Adhyan, Jatimatramar, Samanyas, Sapagrastha, Thampurakkal, Visishta Nambuthiri (Kerala)

Sub-divisions : Adhyam, Apastamba, Asval-ayana, Bhattatiri, Bondhayana, Jatiratra, Samanyas, Tampurakkal, Visishta (Agnihotri and Bhattatiris) [E. Therston]

Surnames : Nambuthiri (Kerala)

Clans/lineages : (Illam) (Kerala)

Gotra : Bhardwaj, Bhargana, Kashyap, Kaushik (All Sages), Samanyasa (oridnary) Srivatsa (Sage), Vasisht (sage), Vishwamitra (Sage) (Kerala)

Bhardwaj, Bhargava, Kaushik in South India, Vasistha, Kashyap (E. Thurston).

(e) Taga

Synonyms : Brahman, Tagu, Tyagi Brahman (Haryana), Tyagi (Uttar Pradesh), Tagah, Tyagi (Delhi).

Groups/ sub groups : Bisa, Dasa (Uttar Pradesh) Bade Tyagi, Chote or Dasa, Tyagi (Delhi)

Titles : Tyagi (Uttar Pradesh)

Gaur, Gautam, Kashyap, Sangtan, Sanil, Tyagi, Vashisht, Vats (Delhi)

Exogamous units/ clans: Bachal, Dikshit (Haryana)

Bhasyan, Gaur, Sangla, Tectwal, Yat (Delhi)

Bachhal, Bais, Bargala, Bisa in North-west Province, Chandel, Chauhan, Dasa, Dikshit, Gaur, Sanadh, Vasisht (W. Crooke),

Got : Bachcla, Bhardwaj, Goutam in Haryana and Punjab, Palair, Saroh (H.A. Rose)

Gotra : Bachas, Bhardwaj, Parasar, Vasisht (Haryana), Bhardwaj, Vasisht, Vishwamitra (Utter Pradesh).

Bhardwaj, Goutam, Kashyap, Sandilya, Vasisht (Delhi).

References

- Communities, Segments, Synonyms, Surnames and Titles by K.S. Singh.
- People of India Series, Vol. VIII, ASI
- Oxford University Press, Delhi-1996.

Bibliography

Aggarwal, Pratap, C., Caste, Religion and Power : An Indian Case Study; Sri Ram Centre for Industrial Relations, New Delhi, 1971.

Ahmed, E. : Bihar : A Physical Economic and Regional Geography, (Ranchi, 1965).

Apte, Mahadev L.I, Region, Religion and Language. Parameters of Identity in the Process of Acultu-ration. The Hague, Mouton Publishers, 1977.

Akinchan, S., "Caste, Class and Politics", 1995, Gyan Publishing House, New Delhi-2.

Barber, Bernard. 'Social Mobility in the Caste System in India, The Hague, Mouton Publishers, 1968.

Beteille, Andre. Castes : Old and New Essays in Social Structure and Social Stratification. Bombay. Asia Publishing House, 1969.

———, Caste, Class and Power, Berkelay : University of California Press, 1969.

———, Caste - Old and New, Bombay : Asia Publishing House, 1969.

Bhatt, S.C., The Encyclopaedic, District-Gazetteers of India, Vol. VIII, Gian Publishing House, Delhi.

Bhattacharya, Jogendra Nath; Hindu Castes and Sects, Munshiram Manoharlal Publisher Pvt. Ltd. 1995.

Bhondel, I., 'Voters, Parties and Leaders : The Social Fabrics of British Politics, London, Rengmin, 1967.

Blunt, EAH; United Province of Agra and Oudh, Census of India, 1931, Part-I & II, USHA Publications, Daryaganj, Delhi, 1987.

Chaudhary, R.K., History of Bihar, Patna, Swatantra Nava Bharat Press, 1958.

Census of India 1901 (U.P. Census), North-West Provinces and Oudh Report.

Census of India, 1931 (Bihar and Orissa) Part - II Report, Vol. VII, USHA Publication, 1987.

Chandra, Bipan, "Nationalism and Colonialism in Modern India, Orient Longmen Ltd., 1979.

Crooke, W. The Tribes and Castes of the North-Western India (Calcutta : Government Printing Press, 1896; rpt. 1974, Delhi: Cosmo Publications, vol. 1.

Das, Arvind N., 'Agrarian Unrest and Socio-Economic Change (1900-1980), Manohar, New Delhi, 1983.

Das, Arvind N., 'The Republic of Bihar, Penguin Books India (P) Ltd, New Delhi, 1992.

Dayal, P. : The Bihar Plain — "A Regional Study" Transcations, Indian Council of Geography, I.G.U. Vol.-5, Dec; 1968.

Diwakar, R.R. (Ed.) : Bihar Through The Ages, Bombay, Orient Longman, 1959.

Dracup, A.H., Sorley, H.T., 'Census of India, 1931' Bombay Presidency (Part I & II Tables) USHA Publication, 1987, New Delhi-2.

Dube, S.C., "Indian Society", NBT, Delhi, 1990.

Dutt, N.K. "Origin and Growth of Caste in India", 1 (1931), II (1965).

Dutta, K.K., Freedom Movement in Bihar, Vol. III, Patna, Govt., of Bihar, 1957 & 1958.

Enthoven, R.E. The Tribes and Castes of Bombay, Vol.1, 1920, Cosmo Publication, Delhi.

Ghurye, G.S. "Caste and Race in India", 1996 (Rpt.), Popular Prakashan Pvt. Ltd. Tardeo, Bombay.

Grover, Virendra and Arora, Ranjana (Ed.) Encyclopaedia of India and Her States", Vol.7, Deep & Deep Publications, 1998, New Delhi-27.

Hauser, Walter; — The Bihar Provincial Kisan Sabha, 1929-1942, University of Chicago, 1961.

Home Ministry, India, 'Causes and Nature of Current Agrarian Tensions, New Delhi, 1969.

Hussain, Majid - Encyclopaedia of India (Bihar), Vol. XXVI, Rima Publishing House, New Delhi-12, 1994.

Hutton, J.H. Census of India 1931, Vol. 2, Gian Publishing House, Delhi - 7.

Ibbetson, Denzil, 'Punjab Castes, Low Price Publications, Delhi (Rpt.) 1993.

Iyer, A. Krishna, L.K., 'The Tribes and Castes of Cochin, Vol. III, Cosmo Publications, New Delhi, 1981.

Kosambi, D.D., "An Introduction to the Study of India History", 1996 (Rpt.), Popular Prakashan Pvt. Ltd., Tardeo, Bombay-34.

Kothari, Rajni (Ed.) Caste in Indian Politics (Caste and Political Recruitment in Bihar), Orient Longman Ltd., 1970.

Lacey, W.G.; Census of India, 1931 (Bihar and Orissa), Part - 1 Report, Vol. VII, USHA Publication, 1987.

Majumdar, D.N., and Madan, T.N.," An Introduction to Social Anthropology, National Publishing House, New Delhi-2, (1988).

Mathur, M.L., 'Encyclopaedia of Backward Castes : Mandal, Media and Aftermath, Kalpaz Publications, Vol. IV, Delhi, 2003.

Mead PJ, and MacGregor Glaird, 'Bombay: Census of India, 1911, Part 1, USHA, 1987.

Mohanti, K.K.; Social Mobility and Caste Dynamics, Rawat Publications, New Delhi - 1993.

Mohanty, P.K.; "Encyclopaedia of Castes and Tribes in India, 2000, Indian Publishers Distributors.

Mungerilal Commission (Bihar) for Backward Classes, 1975, Patna, Bihar (Third Report).

Nesfield, J.C. "Brief view of the Caste System of North-West-Provinces and Oudh, 1855.

Panandiker; V.A. Pai (Ed.) "The Politics of Backwardness" chapter-"Reservation and After: The case of Bihar" by Sachchidananda, 1997, Konark Publishers Pvt. Ltd., Delhi-92.

Risley, H.H., The Tribes and Castes of Bengal (Calcutta : Bengal Secretariat Press, 1891; rpt. 1981, Calcutta Firma Mukhopadhyay, Vol. 1.

Rose, H.A., 'A Glossary of the Tribes and Castes of the Punjab and North-West Frontier Province, Vol. II and III, Asian Educational Services, Delhi, 1990.

Sanskrityayan Rahul, 'Meri Jeevan yatra', Allahabad, 1961.

Saraswati, Swami Sahajanand; Brahmarshi-Vansa-Vistar (Bihta, Bihar : Shri Sitaramashram, 1971) Third Edition.

Saraswati, Swami Sahajanand, 'Mera Jeevan Sangharsh (Hindi), Bihta, 1952.

———, Bhumihar Brahman Parichaya, Benaras, 1916.

———, Brahman Samaj Ki Sthithi, Benaras.

Sharma, Anuradha - Castes and Tribes in India, Commonwealth Publishers, 1998.

Sharma, K.L. (Ed.) "Caste and Class in India" 1998 (Rpt.), Rawat Publications, Jaipur.

Singh K.S., "People of India Series, Gujarat, Part-1, Vol. XXII, 2003, Popular Prakashan Pvt. Ltd., Mumbai.

Singh, K.S., "People of India", Vol-XX, Delhi, Manohar Publishers and Distributors, New Delhi-2.

Singh, K.S., "People of India Series, India's Communities, Vol. 1, Popular Prakashan Pvt. Ltd; Bombay.

Singh, K.S., (Ed.) People of India, Goa, Vol.-XXI, 1993 Popular Prakashan Pvt.; Ltd.; Bombay.

Singh, K.S., "People of India Series, India's Communities, Vol. 1, Popular Prakashan Pvt. Ltd; Bombay.

——— India's Communities,Vol. II. Oxford University Press, Delhi, 1998.

——— India's Communities, Vol. III. Oxford University Press, Delhi, 1998.

Singh, K.S., Bhalla, V. Kaul Vinod, The Biological Variation in Indian Populations, Vol. X, Oxford University press, Delhi, 1994.

Singh, K.S., (Ed.) People of India (Haryana) Vol. XXIII, Manohar, 1994.

Singh, K.S., "People of India (Kerala), Vol. XXVII, ASI.

Sinha, Indradeep, 'Sathi Ke Kisanon Ka Aithasik Sangharsha, Patna, 1969.

Shukla, Kiran – Caste Politics in India, Mittal Publications, Delhi 1987.

Srinivas M.N., Caste in Modern India, Media Promoter

and Publisher Pvt. Ltd., Bombay, 1994.

Thapar, Romila; 'A History of India, 1977, Penguin Books Ltd; England.

Thurston, Edgar and Rangachari, K., 'Castes and Tribes of Southern India, Vol. V, Asian Educational Services, New Delhi, 1993.

Wilson, John, "Indian Caste", Deep Publication, New Delhi, 1976.

Newspaper/Periodicals

Brahmarshi Samaj Magazine (Quarterly) Jan-March, '2003 issue, Kankerbagh, Patna.

Caste in Education, 'Eastern Economist' vol. 39, October 5, 1962.

Caste (The Future Caste) Seminar' 70, papers, June, 1960.

Muslim OBCs : Confronting Inequalities, Economic and Political Weekly, Nov. 15-21, 2003.

Ranveer Sena and 'Massacre Widows'—Sinha, Arvind and Sinha, Indu; —Economic and Political Weekly, October 27, 2001.

The Times of India, Delhi edition, 31st March 2004.

The Times of India, Delhi edition, 17th April 2004.

Glossary

Anthropometric	:	It deals with the identification of the communities on their different physical traits, which differs from community to community.
Anuloma	:	Opposite to Partiloma. (p. 187)
Ayachak	:	Brahmans whose profession is not begging (i.e.; Bhumihar)
Begari	:	In agriculturist society forced labour on agriculture land and allied services are taken by landlords.
Bhumihar/Babhan	:	A jati found in different parts of the country under different names. It's main occupation is agriculture and they scale themselves higher in the jati/ varna system. (only after Brahman)
Caste	:	Term devised by Portuguese to denote several divisions (Jatis)

		in Hindu society, its use is confused many times.
Chhati	:	Observed on 6th days in Hindu's family after birth of the child. Some ceremonies also takes place on this occasion.
Dhanbati	:	This is a symbol of okeying the marriage on the part of bridegroom family in which Paddy is distributed and one part of it is taken away by the bride family members to their house.
Dwarpuja	:	In Bhumihar Brahman, after the arrival of the bridegroom at bride's house, puja is performed by the priest before entering of bride's into the house of groom.
Endogamy	:	The permissibility of marriage only within a specified group; exists in conjunction with exogamy.
Eponym	:	Its being either a vedic saint or a chief of comparatively modern date.
Exogamy	:	The permissibility of marriage only outside a specified group; exists in conjunction with endogamy.
Gotra	:	The members of which profess to be descended from the mythical rishi or inspired saint whose name the gotras beared.
Grihastha	:	Householder, second of four Ashramas.

Halis	:	Farm and Lanes found in Gujarat in olden period.
Infant Marriage	:	In Hindu society and in other religion also, marriage between boys and girls took place very early at the age (say 5 to 13 years).
Jajman	:	A pattern of inter-jati co-operation and dependence in which artisans, craftsmen, and jati with specialised occupations render their services to land-owners for stipulated annual payment in kind usually a quantity of newly harvested crop; there is also exchange of specialized services among these jatis.
Janaue	:	A sacred thread worn by the twice born caste in Hindu society.
Kacchi Food	:	Usually taken by some high castes and also priests in which raw materials foods are provided to them and in many cases they cooked themselves.
Kudumi	:	The tuft of hair tied into a knot hanging over the forehead.
Kul Devta/Devi	:	Clan Male/Female diety.
Lineage	:	Family, Kula etc.;
Magni	:	Marriage Proposal
Mangalsutra	:	Pendant worn by the married women in Hindu society.
Matkora	:	Digging of soil in the night from earth by the bride; a Hindu customs observed during marriage ceremony.

Mour	:	A headgear made of meltalic wires and thread of delicate design, worn by groom.
Muls	:	Exogamous divisions of the territorial type.
Mundan	:	First hair cut.
Nuclear family	:	Domestic unit consisting of husband, wife and their unmarried children.
Pakki food	:	Cooked food such as bread, vegetables.
Partiloma	:	Intermarriages between female members of the higher varnas and males of the lower.
Patkati	:	Observed during marriage ceremony in groom family house in Bhumihar/Babhan.
Polyandry	:	Where a woman has more than one husband at the sametime; in faternal polyandry these are brothers among themselves.
Polygamy	:	Where a person has more than one spouse at the same time.
Purukhs	:	Muls divided into smaller sections are called Purukhs.
Rigveda	:	The earliest literary composition of the Aryans.
Ritual	:	Upper Jatis preserves their state of purity by avoiding physical contact and inter-dinning with lower jatis; concept of pollution and purity is attached with it.
Saptapadi	:	Seven rounds taken by bride's and groom's in front of fire during marriage ceremony.

Sindurdan : Custom perhaps borrowed from the non Aryan race, it is smearing of vermilon on the parting of the bride's hair, in Hindu society.

Sohar : Folksong sung by the ladies of the house in whose house child birth has taken place.

Sub-Caste : A relative term used with reference to caste, for example: in Maratha Brahman and Konkan (Chitpavan) Brahman, the first one would be called a caste while the later would be called sub-caste.

Territorial : It refers either to some very early settlement of a section or to the birth place of its founder, as is found in Babhan sub -caste.

Thali : A marriage pendant and symbol of married women in Nambuthiri.

Totem : Each sept bears the name of an animal, a tree, a plant or some material object natural or artificial which the members of that sept are prohibited from killing, eating, cutting, burning, carrying, laing etc.

Zamindar : Hereditary agent, lowest in feudal hierarchy, from whom state collected land revenue and who in turn collected it from common land-owners and tenants, used in some regious to refer to any owner of agricultural land.

Index

Aboriginal Races-Process of Elevation of the 22

All India Agricultural Labour Enquiry 68

All India Kisan Sabha 101,118

Anavalas/Anavil 134,138

—— Brahmans 136

— of Surat District 139

—— Exogamous gotras 137

—— Followers of Vaishnavite and Shavite Seets 139

—— Important Rituals 15

Anavil Women 138

ANS Institute at Patna 57

Anti-Reservation Stir 96

Anti Zamindari Organisation 101

Athens of India 17

Authority of Sankaracharya 133

Authority of Territorial Class 35

Ayachak Brahman 32

Babhans 34, 35, 43, 47, 51, 53, 56, 71, 76, 78, *et.al*

—— of Bihar 70, 136

—— Distribution of 45, 46-47

—— Marriage Ceremony of 72

——Marriage and Custom Related to 68

—— Origin of the 32

——Religion of 39

Barahia Bakshat Struggle 120

Beames, Dr. 33,53

Bhumihar

——Babhan / Brahman 23, 29, 31, 55

—— Bemwar 39

—— Brahman 23, 31, 32
—— Castes 53
— and Bihar 89
— of Eastern part of the Province 123
— Somatometric Character of the 51
—— Cast Politicians 97
—— *Donawar* 39
—— Families of Bihar 76
—— Gautam 39
—— *Hararia, Kodaria Bhusbarat Domkatar* 41
—— *Kinwar* 38
—— Landholders 57
—— Leaders 95
—— Leteral Meaning of 30
—— Mahasabha 32, 118
—— Thakurs 41
—— Village 162
Bhumihars
—— of Benares 26
—— Bihar 23
—— Caste Organisation of 37
—in Some Lok Sabha Constituencies in Bihar 173-174
Bhumi Sena 102
Big landholders Bhumihar 31
Bihar
—Legislative Assembly 89
—Mixture of Three Languages 25
—Orissa 109
—Pradesh Kisan Sabha 101, 102, 103
—— Unit of C. P. I 120
— and U.P. 55
—— Zamindars 106
Bihari Languages 81
Birth of a Girl Child in Desai Family 137
Birth of a Male Child 76
BJP and Samta Party 105
Blue Blood Chief of Rajasthan 22
Bougle 28
Brahmanical
—— Class 35
—— Community 27
—— Gotra 35-38
—— Titles 23, 36
Brahmans 18, 21, 36, 54
—— Kannaujia 35
—— of Partabgarh 22
—— and Rajput Relations between 41
—— Sarwaria 35
Brahmanised Chief 21-22
Brahmarish' 16
—— Samaj 109, 122
—— Sangh 96
—— Sena and Ranveer Sena 103
Brahmins 108
—— Bhumihar 117
Brihdratha 24

British Period 71
British Rule 136

Cast
——and Agricultural Occupation of Bihar (1951), 67
—— Association 84, 86
—— Based Politics of Bihar 90
—— Based Private Armies 103
——Cardinal Feature of - 28
——Communities, Segments, Synonymous Surnames and Titles of Brahman / Bhumihar Babhan 176-179
——Composition of Bihar Pradesh Congress Executive Committee (1934-62) 92, 93
——Composition of Population 94
—— System of India 55, 60
—— a, System of Inequality 27
——Wise Census Enumeration 48
—— And Education in Bihar 108
—— And Occupation 163
Castes - Four Categories of 27
Castes of the Present Days 21
Centre Core of Bihar 24
Chapekar 129, 131
Chhibar, Mati Das 141
Chief Territorial Sub-Divisions of Bhumihar 38-41
Chiefly Agricultural Class 31
Chitpavan
—— Brahmans of Deccan 132
—— Brahmans of Goa 133
Chitpavans 128-131
Chitpalan, old name of Chitpavan 127
Christian Missionary 19
Civil Marriage Rule 72
Commercial Traveller 17
Communities in India 49
Colleges in the named of Bhumihars 175
Connubium 18
—— and Social Life- Rules of 20
Court of Santrocottus 18
Creation of Bihar and Orissa 89
Crooke 123

Delhi Development Authority 126
Descendents of the Second and Third Castes 18
Determination of Occupation of a Caste 55
Different aspects of Bhumihar Castes 159

Different Linguistic Belt of Bihar 159
Defferent Castes MLA an Different Assembly Election 90
Disposal of the Dead 77
"Dispossessed' Sections of Bihar Society 110
Distribution of Tyagi 127
Districts of Undirided Bihar 114
Division of Bihar Universities 108
Dominant Castes and Ascendent Castes 107
Dravidian Brahman 144
Dumont Louis 88
Dumonts's "Horno Hierarchicus" 27

Eastern Parts of U.P. 81
Edict of Asoka 18
Educated Class of Indians 108
Education Mafias 116
Educational Institutions 109
Elite Cultivating Castes in U.P. 45
Elliot, Sir H.M. 35, 122
Emergence of Sub - Caste 15
Eminent Literatteurs 82
Endogamous Groups 124, 126, 143
Essence of Caste 28
Existence of Bhumihar Class 34
Exogmous *Gotras* 125,148
Exogamy and Endogamy 62, 75, 79

Factors for Erosion of the Family and Kinship in Bihar 158
Famous Local Saints 20
Features of Hindu Caste Society 28
Feeling of Caste Solidarity 85
Fernandes, George 95
Folk Arts of Bhumihars 158
Followers of Arya Samaj 127
Followers of Sankaracharya 132
Foremost Leaders of Peasantry in Bihar 118
Forsyth, Captain 22
Foundation of Kisan Organisation in Bihar 119

Gandhiji 109, 118
Gaur Brahmins 123
General Elections of Beghu Sarai Constituency 98-99
Ghazipur Branch of Bhumihar 34
Ghazipur District in Eastern U.P. 118
Ghurye, G.S. Indian Sociologist 88
'Gohar' 105

'Gotra' Complex 131, 132
Gough 29
Grierson, Dr. 25,72, 77
Gujariti Brahman 134

Hararia, Kadaria, Bhusbarat, Domkatar 41
Hauser, Walter 95
Heriditary Guild of Caste System 19
Herodotus 19
Hindi Speaking Region of India- Integral Part of the 25
Hindu Law 74
—— of Inheritance 143
Hindu Religion 170
Hindu Society 171, 172
—— Castes of 16
—— Frame work of 170
Hindus of India - Caste System of 29
Hislop, Mr. 21
Historical Development of Caste 18

Ibbetson, Mr. 19
Indentification of the community and their listing 49
Immigrant Brahmins 123
Important Caste of Landowner and Agriculturalists 31
Important Cultivating and Landowning Caste 122
Important Function of a Caste System 171
Important Marriage Rituals 75
Independence Movement 106
Indian Feudal System 30
Iyer, 144, 145

Jajmani System 57, 167
"Jammu and Kashmir" 141
Janamejaya 122, 123
Jati Panchayat 158
Jha, B.N. 90
Jones, Morris 83
Jujhotia Brahman 41

Kannojia origin 41
Kayasthas 23, 53, 68, 87, 91, 110, 171
—— and Bhumihars 106
Ketkar 28
Khare, R.S. 86
Khet Mazdoor Sabha 121
Kisan Leaders of Bihar 119
Kothari, Rajni 86, 87, 88

Lacedaemonians 19
Lacy, W.G. 42
Large and Influential Caste in Bihar 23
Leach, 28

Leading Supporters of Rebels 106
Leaders of Kisan Sabha 121

Magadh 24
Magadhi Languages 81
Mahabrahmans 34
Maharani of Tekari 71
Maine, Sir 69
Maithili Brahmanas 78
Maithili, Magadhi and Bhojpur Languages 25
Mandal, B.P. 91
Manu's Castes 16-17
—— Views about 17
—"Institutes" 18, 20
Marriage and Custom Related to Babhan 68
Marriage Procession of Bride-groom 74
Mastans and Bhatelas 134,
—— origins of the 135
Marx, Karl and Thorston Veblen 84
Max Muller, Prof. 79
Mathura 143
Melennan, Mr. J.F 68
Meghasthenes 18
Mishra, B.B. 108
Monogamy, 75, 143, 148, 153
Mutability of Castes 20

Nambuthiri 144, 149, 151
—— Festivals 154
—— Main Natural Resource 152
—— Sub-Division of the 146-148
—— Traditional Occupation of the 154
—— Women 145, 149, 154
—— Yogakshema Sabha 152-154
Nationalist Struggle in Bihar Story of the 100
Natural Crises 19
NDA 97
Nesfield, Mr. 22, 29, 71
Non-Cooperation Movement 120, 121
North India-Brahman in 171
North-Western Provinces 70
Nuclear Families 149, 154

Occupation of Babhan Caste 55
Oja, Saryug, Prominent Freedom Fighter 165
Old Rituals 80
Oldham. Dr. 34
Organisation of Bhumihars 37
Origion of Bhumihar Caste 29
Origions of Muhials 140, 141
Orthodox Hindu Caste 29

Pandey, Ramakant 165
Pandit, Yadunandan Sharma 119

Panikkar, K.M. & Majid Siddiqui 104
Peasant Movement 100
—— Caste Colour of 102
—— in Central Bihar 101
—— Linkage between National 104
People of Bhumihar Society 157
Politics of Bihar 91
Polygamy 126, 148
—— and Poliandry 133
Population of Bhumihar (Babhan) in the Country, Census (1931), 42
Powerful Figure in Politics in Bihar 119
Process of Fusion of Castes 88
Process of Marriage 72-79

Qualitative Aspect of Exogamic Integration 131

Radical Leaders in Bihar Politics 101
Rahul Sankrityayana 121
Raja Bhagwant Rai of Asothar 23
Raja Manik Chand 22
Rajputs 54, 68
—— and Kayasthas 59, 70, 89
Rampai and Domkatar Sections 70
Ranveer Sena 104, 105, 156
—— Stronghold of 168
Remarriage of a Widower 75
Rigveda 27
Rise in Caste Tension 157
Risley 128
Rose 125
Rules of Exogamy 37
Rural Areas of Patna 102

Saivas and Saktas 54, 80
Sandilya Eponimus Section 36
Saraswati Swami Sahajanand 16, 25, 30, 32, 85, 96, 100, 101, 109, 118, 119
Sharma, Karyanand 120
Sherring, Mr. 38
Singh, Kapildeo 109, 165
—— U.P. (former PM) 95
Sinha, A.N. 90
Siviha, S.K. 25, 89, 90, 101
—— and Mahatma Gandhi 106, 107
—— M.P. 90
— and K.B. Sahay 90
Skandapurana 129
Slayer of Kshtriyas 127
Social Status of the Caste 53
'Society for Social Health Care" 109
Soil of the Gangetic Valley 54
South Eastern Bihar 53
South Gangetic Plain 24

Sraddh Ceremony 78
Srinivas, M.N. 83, 100
Symbols of Married Women 75

Taga in Haryana 124
Taga/Tyagi in U.P. 122, 123
—— Community 126
Tenure Holders of all Qrades 56
Territorial and Eponimons System 37
Thakur, C.P. Dr. 96, 104, 115
Town of Vapi 137
Town of Bihar 15
Trading Town of North Bihar 97
Traditional Occupation of Mohyal 144
True Origin of Bhumihar 35
Tyagi of Delhi 125

Undivided Bihar 81
Upanayan Rituals 54
Upper Castes 110, 115
—— in Bihar 57
—— Students 109
Upper Doab Region 46

Vaidehas 17
Vaishnavas 54
Vaishnavism 79
Verna Hierarchy 28
Verna Loyalty 156
Viswamitra 20
Vishwanath Peshwa Balaji 127, 128

Well Known Rajputs 35
Women of Kahar Caste 72

Yadav, Laloo Prasad 96
Yadav. Sh R.K. of R.J.D. 96
Year (1981), 102
Year (2003) 96
Younger Generation 158, 164

Zamindars 24
—— in the Pre-Colonial & Colonial Times 56
Zamindari
—— Abolition of 56, 100, 101
—— Legal Death of 119

❑❑❑